Volume 3

Experiencing God

Eberhard Arnold

PLOUGH PUBLISHING HOUSE

Published by Plough Publishing House
Walden, New York, USA
Robertsbridge, East Sussex, UK
Elsmore, NSW, Australia

Plough is the publishing house of the Bruderhof, an international community of families and singles seeking to follow Jesus together. Members of the Bruderhof are committed to a way of radical discipleship in the spirit of the Sermon on the Mount. Inspired by the first church in Jerusalem (Acts 2 and 4), they renounce private property and share everything in common in a life of nonviolence, justice, and service to neighbors near and far. To learn more about the Bruderhof's faith, history, and daily life, see Bruderhof.com.

Translated from the 1936 edition of *Innen Land: Ein Wegweiser in die Seele der Bibel und in den Kampf um die Wirklichkeit* (Buchverlag des Almbruderhof e. V.). This edition is based on the 1975 English edition translated by Winifred Hildel and Miriam Potts.

Cover image: *Radiant Clouds* (oil on canvas) by Erin Hanson, copyright © Erin Hanson. Used with permission.

A catalog record for this book is available from the British Library. Library of Congress Cataloging-in-Publication Data

Names: Arnold, Eberhard, 1883-1935, author.
Title: Experiencing God / Eberhard Arnold.
Other titles: Erleben des Gottesfriedens. English
Description: Walden, New York, USA : Plough Publishing House, 2020. |
Series: Inner land: a guide into the heart of the gospel ; 3 | Includes bibliographical references.
Identifiers: LCCN 2019045348 (print) | LCCN 2019045349 (ebook) | ISBN 9780874862966 (hardback) | ISBN 9780874862973 (ebook)
Subjects: LCSH: Spirituality--Christianity. | Experience (Religion) | Peace--Religious aspects--Christianity.
Classification: LCC BV4501.3 .A75613 2020 (print) | LCC BV4501.3 (ebook) | DDC 248.4--dc23
LC record available at https://lccn.loc.gov/2019045348
LC ebook record available at https://lccn.loc.gov/2019045349

Printed in the United States

Dedicated to my faithful wife,
Emmy Arnold

Contents

When anyone is united to Christ, there is a new world; the old order has gone, and a new order has already begun.

2 Corinthians 5:17 (NEB)

Preface

Born to an academic family in the Prussian city of Königsberg, Eberhard Arnold (1883–1935) received a doctorate in philosophy and became a sought-after writer and speaker in Germany. Yet like thousands of other young Europeans in the turbulent years following World War I, he and his wife, Emmy, were disillusioned by the failure of the establishment – especially the churches – to provide answers to the problems facing society.

In 1920, out of a desire to put into practice the teachings of Jesus, the Arnolds turned their backs on the privileges of middle-class life in Berlin and moved to the village of Sannerz with their five young children. There, with a handful of others, they started an intentional community on the basis of the Sermon on the Mount, drawing inspiration from the early Christians and the sixteenth-century Anabaptists. The community, which supported itself by agriculture and publishing, attracted thousands of visitors and eventually grew into the international movement known as the Bruderhof.

Eberhard Arnold's magnum opus, *Inner Land* absorbed his energies off and on for most of his adult life. Begun in the months before World War I, the first version of the book was published in 1914 as a patriotic pamphlet for German soldiers titled *War: A Call to Inwardness*. The first version to carry the title *Inner Land* appeared after the war in 1918; Arnold had extensively revised the text in light of his embrace of Christian pacifism. In 1932 Arnold began a new edit, reflecting the influence of religious socialism and his immersion in the writings of the sixteenth-century Radical Reformation, as well as his experiences living in the Sannerz community. Arnold continued to rework the book during the following three years, as he and the community became targets of increasing harassment as opponents of Nazism. The final text, on which this translation is based, was published in 1936. Arnold had died one year earlier as the result of a failed surgery.

This final version of *Inner Land* was not explicitly critical of the Nazi regime. Instead, it attacked the spirits that fed German society's support for Nazism: racism and bigotry, nationalistic fervor, hatred of political enemies, a desire for vengeance, and greed. At the same time, Arnold was not afraid to critique the evils of Bolshevism.

The chapter "Light and Fire," in particular, was a deliberate public statement at a decisive moment in Germany's history. Eberhard Arnold sent Hitler a copy on November 9, 1933. A week later the Gestapo raided the community and ransacked the author's study. After the raid, Eberhard Arnold had two Bruderhof members pack the already printed signatures

of *Inner Land* in watertight metal boxes and bury
them at night on the hill behind the community
for safekeeping. They later dug up *Inner Land* and
smuggled it out of the country, publishing it in Lich-
tenstein after Eberhard Arnold's death. Emmy Arnold
later fulfilled her husband's wish and added marginal
Bible references. (Footnotes are added by the editors.)

At first glance, the focus of *Inner Land* seems to
be the cultivation of the spiritual life. This would be
misleading. Eberhard Arnold writes:

> These are times of distress; they do not allow us
> to retreat just because we are willfully blind to the
> overwhelming urgency of the tasks that press upon
> human society. We cannot look for inner detachment
> in an inner and outer isolation. . . . The only thing
> that could justify withdrawing into the inner self
> to escape today's confusing, hectic whirl would be
> that fruitfulness is enriched by it. It is a question
> of gaining within, through unity with the eternal
> powers, that strength of character which is ready to
> be tested in the stream of the world.

Inner Land, then, calls us not to passivity, but to
action. It invites us to discover the abundance of a
life lived for God. It opens our eyes to the possibilities
of that "inner land of the invisible" where "our spirit
can find the roots of its strength." Only there, says
Eberhard Arnold, will we find the clarity of vision we
need to win the daily battle that is life.

The Editors

The Experience of God

Historical events must lead us to faith

The more shaking the historical events of a time period, the more necessary it is to recognize what spiritual power determines their course. Outward events as violent as those of our day call for an insight into this ultimate will and its aim. But the more agitated the times, the more temporary matters push to the fore. At such times of tension, a tangle of issues seems to prevent any clarity about the ultimate answer. Mounting pressure leads to emergency measures that seem imperative. Conditioned to the times, they are not able to turn the tide of need and distress. One attempt follows another, misery increases, and nothing can overcome it; people go under in the day-to-day struggle and lose all hope of a change.

Some think we have to give first place to patriotic ideas and the historic task laid on the nation. The longed-for freedom of the national community appears imperative at the moment, demanding that everything else be subjected and sacrificed to this.

Others, however, believe in a historical development to raise to power in every nation all those oppressed and exploited by competition and private enterprise; for a time they are to be given unlimited power. In comparison with both of these, the champions of liberty and freedom for the individual (with the consequent competition) retreat into the background. No state protection preserves them from their approaching insignificance. What falls almost completely by the wayside in the struggle for quickly-won power is this: in the end, a classless society based on justice and peace shall unite all extremes.

Not one of these three directions with their struggles and fluctuating hopes expects anything from the prophetic power of the Christ-proclamation. Those who stand in the middle between the first two extremes have no fear that their egotistical life might be shattered by the kingdom of God. And where individuals try to comply with the economic system, their consciences become too dull to be aware of how universal need and distress are. But to the right and to the left, people think more seriously. To the right, in contradiction to Christ, they want religion to uphold unconditionally the power structure they have fought for. Christian consciences are meant to surrender to it in willing submission; the conscience becomes the slave of political power. To the left, all they see in the Christian confession is their most hated opponent. All they know of Christianity is the social power of class privilege, which, also in contradiction to Christ, covers up social injustice with a hypocritical mien and refers the tormented to a better world hereafter. The Christian conscience appears to represent the height of injustice and should be exterminated.

To all this, Christian confessions in general, apart from a few rare exceptions, have nothing to say. The prophetic clarity of intense and confident waiting for a final kingdom – a kingdom of loving community in God – has given way to feeble imitations. People no longer believe that the peace, justice, and brotherliness of the kingdom of God are a present reality that eclipses all other hopes of the future. And yet all these prospects of a better future are borrowed from and would not exist without the hopes of prophetic early Christianity. But not even the historical significance of early Christian prophecy is taken seriously. In practice, the general run of Christianity just accepts existing conditions of social order, or disorder, including any new ideas people come up with. The early Christian expectation is being forgotten. Because it is no longer seriously believed, it has, for present-day Christianity, lost the dynamic to overturn and transform everything.

Rom. 12:1–2

There are still those who point out seriously that God is quite other than man, quite other than all man of himself wants or does.[1] But there are very few who believe in this quite different God so truly that they see the approach of his reign and comprehend it. Only these very few lend a hand in faith so that a fundamental change that will affect everyone and all conditions actually begins. The inner thinking born of faith in God's kingdom is completely other than the thinking of human religion: those with faith in God's kingdom approach everything with a certainty from God himself that the impossible can become

---

1 Reference to the theologian Karl Barth, 1886–1968. In the following paragraphs, Arnold contrasts Barth's concept of the otherness of God (*totaliter aliter*) with pantheistic thought.

possible, in outer circumstances just as much as in
the innermost. This faith in God may be as small as
a grain or seed, yet it will remove obstacles of the
weightiest nature.

Such faith lets what belongs to the future and to
the beyond penetrate the present – this earth. Out
of the strength it derives from this source, it sets to
and gives everything shape and form. The believer
has realized that to leave God in the world beyond is
to deny Christ. For Christ has said and proved that
God draws near, so near that everything has to be
changed. "Change from the very foundation. For the
reign of God has drawn near. Believe in these tidings
of joy!" Yet Jesus knew that this triumphant joy would
be accepted by only a very few. People are readier to
place their faith in the autonomy of things than in
the message of God that overturns everything. They
experience things more forcibly than they experience
God. They are idolaters, for they serve the creature
more than the Creator. Here faith has to step in and
unite our life with the creative power. This power
alone remains superior to any created power.

God remains God, but we become his
God stands above all that happens. Only when we
are one with God can our faith withstand all powers
that storm it. It is not we who stand firm. Only God is
invincible. In him alone is that freedom of soul found
that saves us from being enslaved, however mighty
the enslaving power. God has drawn near. We can be
in God. God wants to be known and experienced. Yet
we quake before it. The experience of God is terrifying, because it discloses truth. Because God's light
shows up our darkness, we are afraid of it.

Luke 1:34–38

Matt. 17:20

Heb. 11:1–3

Mark 1:15

Matt. 22:14

Rom. 1:25

John 3:19–21

Eph. 5:6–15

God begins – that is the end for man. When in fear
and trembling we know God and are known by him,
God is drawing near to us in person. When the Most
High descends to us, the degraded, he tears away all
cloaks and barriers. God is revealed only through
this fearful experience. When we experience God, Exod. 15:11–16
we appear before him as we are. As long as we shrink
from being exposed for what we are, from God's
unhindered recognition of us, we remain lost and
helpless, overwhelmed by the superior power of the
external world. As long as we submit to things as they
are and remain their slaves, terror of God repels us
and keeps us at a distance.

God is indeed other than we are. It is true that in
our unbelief, he is far removed. We have lost sight of
his image. But it was not always like this and must not Gen. 1:27
stay so. We were created once to be near to him. God
began – that was the beginning for man. There was
a time when God's drawing near did not spell terror.
God's image was once entrusted to us so the Spirit
would rule. This rule of God's Spirit was to be recognized among us as the creative power of unity, as love
and community. We have forfeited all this. We have
lost God. Only God himself could give us back what Gen. 3
we have lost: himself and his image. In Jesus Christ
he did this. In Jesus, God's heart has come into our 2 Cor. 5:19
midst once more. Once more it became clear in Jesus John 3:16
what kind of will and spirit God is. Jesus revealed
afresh what purpose and what reality of unity and
love live in God. He came to do the will of the Father. John 4:34
He brought the Father down to us. He carries out his
decree. He and the Father are one. In Jesus, God is John 10:30
near once more. This message has to be believed.

When Jesus brings God near, God can be recog-
John 7:17 nized as God, and men become men. God's approach
changes us without us becoming God. We stand
in terror before God who is quite other; even in
the gift of his presence, one decisive thing remains
unchanged: we cannot become God. We remain other
John 1:12–14 than God. But God becomes man in order to become
1 Tim. 2:5 our God. God begins – this is the new beginning for
man as man. This experience of God in Christ is
poles apart from any nature mysticism that deifies
man. Such ideas are a delusion: they lead people to
fancy they can merge into some humanistic concep-
tion of one divine All. For Jesus and his apostles,
however, the living God is the other spirit who has to
John 9:39 judge our spirit. As the Law and the Prophets testify,
he is the good and the just, the pure and the holy one.
But we are not good, not just, not pure, and not holy.
God's nature is the opposite of our nature.

God is spirit and God is will in a way that we are
not. He is the will of what is good and perfect. This
Matt. 5:3 we are not. Yet his judgment is our salvation. Out of
the rubble of our degenerate lives he wants to salvage
the life of the creation. God demolishes our nature
as it is and with it the way we have lived and carried
on. Out of these ruins, he wants to bring to light the
human race as it originally was and is finally meant
to be. We are lying under the mountain. The boulders
are being blasted. The debris must be cleared away.
The vein of gold cannot be laid bare unless the mountain is blasted. This freeing is love. The place for
gold is in the sun; without the sun, gold is as black as
coal. God is merciful to us in our poverty, for we are
suffering under it, burdened by it, and buried in it in

spirit and in will. He releases us from every need and
supplies all we lack.   Matt. 11:28

As the will of a power that liberates and a gift
that exposes our true nature, God has drawn near.
He accomplishes this in Christ. He is the God of
uniting love for people who without him are not free,
not united, and not loving. He leads to a future that
allows his will, as his Spirit, to rule over everything
else. God's future wishes to rule over us here and   Matt. 6:10
now. Through this we will be transformed and made   Eph. 2:1–9
true. His kingdom of unity shall take possession of
everything that has been disunited. Here is Christ:
God remains God, we become people of God.

We cannot be merged with God as a drop is
merged with the ocean or a spark with a sea of fire,
for we are not part and parcel of his nature. He is not
the bigger sea of life that encompasses our own small
existence. There is no "we" between us and God.
There is only "Thou." But there *is* this "Thou," and
that is greater. God goes out to us, and a personal
community between "Thou" and "thou" is the result.[2]
It is a moral relationship of unity in will and deed
between God and man. Just this is so unspeakably
great in Jesus Christ: unity becomes a reality in that
the truth is unveiled. The light of truth shines on
us in all its sharpness. When we experience God in   John 8:32
Jesus Christ, we experience his nature as holiness – a
holiness that judges our sin yet draws us into unity
with him. God makes us conscious of our corrupt
state as unholy unrighteousness yet leads everything
to holy righteousness.

---

2 Reference to the ideas of Jewish philosopher Martin Buber, 1878–1965,
   describing the relationship between a human being and God; see Buber,
   Ich und Du, 1923.

Because God is a creative spirit, he cannot let his
works come to a standstill when he has brought us
to realize with horror our own unrighteousness. It is
quite a lot, even a great deal, to know ourselves condemned and absolutely opposed to God and hostile
to him in our own nature, in our actions, and in all
the relationships that condition what we do. But it is
not enough, not nearly enough. First it has to become
clear that we (with all we have and do) are absolutely
different from God and his works, absolutely different
from how he wants us to be. Then his Spirit, who
1 John 1:9   makes all things new, insists that we with all our
Ps. 32:5   doings become at long last as God means us to be.
Our own works have to stop in order for his work to
1 Cor. 11:31–32   begin in us and with us.

Whoever rejects faith in the intervention of God
in his creation here and now as a mystical faith based
on personal experience, whoever cannot believe
that God makes himself known as a living God in
the hearts and lives of those who receive him, has
forgotten the gospel as Matthew, Mark, Luke, and,
in a special way, John passed it on. Such people
deny the power of God as it was revealed in Jesus.
Whoever wants to exalt the limited theological
thinking of the human brain as the only faith to be
experienced rejects unity with God and the works of
love springing from faith, not only for our time and
our contemporaries but also for the apostles of Jesus
Christ and therefore Jesus himself. And whoever
1 John 4:2–3   rejects Jesus rejects God, who sent him.

By bringing God near to us, by coming himself
with power, Jesus exposed our smallness and hostility
John 3:30–36   more clearly than all human dialectic can do. So one
thing is and remains right about these theological

reflections, something fundamental with regard to the Gospels: faced with God's greatness we become terrifyingly aware of our smallness. This absolute feebleness and smallness applies as much to our feeling, willing, and doing as to our thinking.

In God's light our baseness and smallness, our weakness and darkness, must constantly be exposed to him and to ourselves. We can appear before him only as we really are. In his presence, the last shreds of self-idolatry, self-redemption, and self-seeking vanish. His sunshine reveals our life as night. His clarity opens our darkened eyes to see the mountains of filth that bury us. His loving justice shows up the injustice of our rule with its mammonistic nature. His all-inclusive will for peace reveals the will to murder and the urge to set limits that characterize all our ideals. Whether they are based on individualism, patriotism, proletarianism, or any other "ism" makes little difference. God's truth and God's essential nature throw into sharp relief the untruthfulness and insignificance of our lives, private and public.

1 John 1:6–7

1 John 2:9–11

1 John 4:4–16

God's judgment and forgiveness

The experience of God unites and divides at the same time. The deeper his love leads into community with his heart and into the brotherly uniting of people, the more sharply do we become aware of the absolute difference between our sin, which is separation, and his purity, which is unity. There is all the difference in the world between God and man. God wants unity without glossing over the differences.

Uniting with God is possible only through the radical destruction of all powers that oppose God, of everything in conflict with him or done in antagonism to him. Therefore, fundamental in any experience of God is the forgiveness and remission of sin. Forgiveness is the taking away of what is given up (that is, sin). When God unites, what is against him cannot be present. He wants absolute purity in uniting. Therefore everything that opposes purity must first be given up and then taken away. That is forgiveness. God's kingdom will not come without it.

Whoever accepts God in Jesus, or receives in Jesus the forgiveness and the works of God, embraces God himself directly. The faith of the heart embraces God, for God himself has gripped the heart. But God never divides himself when he gives himself to us. He gives himself completely. Acute consciousness of our utter insignificance, dividedness, and sinfulness makes it possible to accept the completely other and eternally indivisible one. The believer is completely one with God, because God alone is complete and one. Faith is truth, for it holds to God. Because God is truth, our self-deception vanishes before him. The heart knows only too well: my small "I" has not been merged into the great "I." Still less has this very small "I" become something great. Lightning from above has shown up the span: the human heart remains a very small "I," and that very small "I" dedicates its will to God completely and worships the great "Thou" that gives itself to us in ineffable loving-kindness.

The believer does not surrender his feeble consciousness to the almighty Consciousness. In experiencing God, Christians are not seeking an opiate for their intelligence. They do not see in the Spirit of God a fading-out of human senses. But just as little do they presume to comprehend the Spirit of

Acts 26:18

God through their powers of understanding. They do not believe they can know God through the insight of their own thinking. Believers do not presume to think they can grasp God through the intensity of their inner life, their emotions, or their willpower. Their faith places God's greatness before them as something so inviolable that feeble human strength has no chance of touching him. All human efforts to achieve union with God are in vain. If faith were a human function, it would be nothing. It could have nothing but a human object; it could never grasp God.

At this point, however, God intervenes. The union so impossible for us ever to achieve takes place through his intervention. If the word "faith" is to keep its meaning, it must be a certainty about what God – not humans but really God – is and does. Faith belongs to God; it does not stem from us. It is God who gives us faith and brings it about. We are one with God only in that faith which is God's affair.

2 Cor. 3:5

In the soul, faith is expressed in a heart-to-heart relationship with others that God brings about. In this uniting of people through faith, God is the one who wills, the one at work. Faith is expressed in an active and effective love in outward circumstances and public life, but it is God at work. God is the loving and active one in these new works of ours.

We believe – and then we do what God is, wills, and works. Faith is something only God can give. Without God, faith is nothing. Wherever community is given through faith, its works are vital and effective because they are God's works. Through faith, God's power is revealed in human weakness, God's greatness in human smallness.

John 15:5

John 6:27–28

God's greatness confronts our smallness

In every decisive experience, our insignificance is confronted with God's greatness, our inadequacy with God's mightiness, our incapacity with God's power. This experience of God runs through the whole history of humankind: God's supremacy overpowering human power. When we stand in reverence before God, our first, intuitive experience of him is of an almighty power before which all human strength is a mere nothing.

Elijah and other early prophets veiled their heads in shuddering awe when God was about to draw near to them. The thought of seeing God fills all genuine people with terror. In the time of the prophets, the sight of God cast the beholder to the ground and killed him. For all reverent ages, the mystery of God's greatness has been awesome beyond measure. Whenever an overpowering sense of this comes over us, all human powers are conquered, just as once the grim and powerful beast of chaos was cast down and conquered. We are bound to shake with terror whenever God draws near.

God's greatness, majesty, and might are beyond all our powers of imagination. If we were to see God, we would perish, because God is so far beyond our capacity to see him face to face. With whom could we compare God? How could we give a picture of this inconceivable greatness and power? God is unattainably great and glorious. The prophets know very well that beside him no other power can endure. His divine decree can never be fulfilled by anything human. No human power can stand before him. The life of God goes far beyond all boundaries of

Rom. 11:33–36

Acts 9:1–9

1 Kings 19:13

Exod. 33:20

Rev. 20:10

Ps. 22:27–31

beginning and end. It towers immeasurably above all created things.

God has power over all nations on earth. He gains authority over all human powers. He will eventually rule over all worlds. Such an overpowering greatness of majesty makes corresponding demands that are unspeakably serious. Those gripped by prophecy sense with awestruck reverence the inviolable and adamant nature of this overwhelming will. As Job had to lay his hand on his mouth, we have to be silent before the greatness of this power. Job 40:4

We sense God's greatness in creation

The greatness and majesty of God is so overwhelming that the whole earth along with all humankind will become his footstool – the footstool on which God's foot rests. Under God's feet lies everything that is visible and invisible. In human eyes, creation is overwhelmingly great and supremely powerful, a shatteringly magnificent prospect through which God draws near to our small human hearts. In the childlike minds of primeval people, God is never confused with nature. The earliest beginnings of faith are far from deifying nature. But childlike people do not experience God's majesty and greatness without nature. They cannot disregard creation when they stand before the Creator. In the mysterious coherence of created worlds, we as believing creatures sense the might of the Creator, who gives all created things their greatness, life, coherence, and unity. In nature, we in our smallness have an intimation of God in his greatness. Isa. 66:1

Rom. 1:19–20

Here we have to pause for a moment. In the rush of a life cut off from nature, we must remember – we must stop and take it in – how overwhelmingly God's power comes to meet us in nature. No scientific progress has changed this mighty fact. The whole history of humankind proves it. Through the great and visible creation, the infinitely greater and invisible nature of God dawns on our insignificance. Creation makes known the power and divinity of the Creator.

Ps. 19
Ps. 104

If we live on the land, the terrors of the powers of nature above all else bring us to quake before God's might. In earthquakes and volcanic eruptions, huge mountains melt like wax beneath God's feet. Thunder and lightning, storm and tempest, scorching desert wind and blazing fire are powerful signs of the awe-inspiring approach of his greatness. Whatever the mighty phenomena of nature, it is the greatness and majesty of God that shakes us. The created world has elemental power. But we sense that over and above it all stands God, the creator who is infinitely greater and mightier than the greatest powers of creation.

Ps. 97:3–5

As God's creations, we quake before these superior forces, but no less before the tremendous mystery of life. Truly reverent people sense an ultimate mystery in all living things, aware that the living, creative Spirit must be greater than all created life. Full of wonder, they stand in awed reverence at the tree bursting with life, at the lively bubbling spring, under the light- and life-dispensing constellations of day and night, and in the midst of earth's fruitfulness and life. How great and powerfully alive God must be to create and sustain all this life! Every deeply shaken and moved heart is struck by the challenge that God, the great creator, must become undisputed sovereign over all this power and life.

God guides human history

In the midst of nature, human history also reveals the overwhelming power of God, both as violent, wrath-filled terrors and as the life-giving, uniting power of love. Awaking to a sense of this with trembling awe, we look back to the beginnings of human history. The profoundly mysterious beginning of the human race comes from God. God also has the end of the human race in his hand. Without God, the end is shrouded from human eyes in the same darkness as the beginning.

Ps. 107

The mystery of God the creator is experienced in all living things, but particularly in the life of human beings. It is the same in the middle as it is at the beginning and the end of the way: God is always drawing terrifyingly near when death and catastrophe break in, as in the destruction of the world in the Flood or the division into nations at the peak of Babel's civilization. In the history of humankind, as in the whole of nature, it is God who is breaking in with mighty power when people are shaken by terrifying events. When God's greatness strikes nations to the ground, empires and world powers are the instruments of his wrath. All the nations of the world must come to fall at the feet of the God of all worlds.

Gen. 6–7

Gen. 11

The Creator of the universe rules over all ages with his decree. In history as in nature, coherence of life, community of life, peace, unity, and life itself shall be revealed (in spite of all opposition) as God's nature and God's power. So God appears to the prophetic eye as the leader and shepherd of history. He guides the history of humankind toward the one goal: that all nations are united in one fold.

Jer. 31:10

John 10:16

Thus the people of Israel experienced God as the God of history in all world events, in all the whirlpools of international politics, and in the collapse of whole peoples. Only God the creator has right and might over all peoples. Whatever may happen, God is arising and claiming the world dominion that is by right his alone. This creative Spirit must – by leading through terrors toward unity – become the God of the universe.

Deut. 32:39–43

As humankind develops, its dawning perception finds the same traces of God in history as in nature. When the conscious mind wins through to greater clarity, it turns to history. It cannot find peace until it has wrested the ultimate meaning from past and present events and those yet to come. To be clear, this awaking faith never confuses God and history (as if the course of events could be God himself), yet God is never experienced without history. Behind all the shattering events in history, awakening people sense God. Gripped by faith, they see God at work, intervening and ultimately determining everything, behind all the mysteriously tangled threads of history, behind every event, great or small. God is at work in all that happens. His majesty towers above all history.

Acts 17:24–31

On this way of faith, Jesus Christ shines out in prophecy and in the apostolic mission: Jesus, the decisive point of all history for the whole of creation! Through Christ, our eye of faith is opened. We see to what extent creation belongs to God and also how far it is estranged from God. And we acquire a discerning eye for history – to what extent it is God's history and also how far it has turned from God and is

hostile to him. Faith catches sight of the coming hour
of decision. In Jesus Christ, prophetic truth becomes
reality. Those illuminated by him see the approach of   Luke 2:34
the kingdom of God as a historical event. The Creator
breaks in upon his degenerate creation. The Lord of
all worlds draws near to history with all its devious
ways. Jesus Christ intervenes in history and turns it
into the history of the end time.

The end goes back to the beginning. The morning
star of the new beginning appears. The secret of life is   2 Pet. 1:19
the sun of the future. God's aim is not the destruction
of all things; his ultimate will is the resurrection of
life. Resistant humankind must go through judgment,
death, and collapse. In the fire of judgment, the
beginning of the new shines out as the end of the old.   Rev. 2:26–28
Renewal and restoration are revealed as the goal of all   1 Cor. 15
that happens. The experience of God is resurrection   Rev. 20
from the dead.

The small world of the individual is meant to
mirror the great world of God's history. To experience God means to give ourselves to the goal of his
kingdom in such a way that we accept his death
sentence and believe in his resurrection. Strength   Phil. 3:8–11
from the future comes to the believer. The Spirit of
the coming Christ is at work and charges us now with
the task of the future. In the reawakening of faith,
the prophetic spirit works toward the establishment
of God's kingdom. New life begins here at this given   Acts 1:8
place and at this very moment. The nature of the
coming kingdom is to be represented in the midst of
the course of history here on this earth.

Through the experience of God, people living
today will be drawn into the end history of creation.

The fire baptism of God's judgment will raise the phoenix from the ashes. The dying of the old world announces the rising of the new. When the human heart is touched by God, it is close to death because new life is coming. Christ's death brings resurrection. The false life, which bears the seeds of death within it, comes to an end. The life that rises in God begins and presses on to the future.

Matt. 24

1 John 3:14

With Christ we too rise to new life

In Persian mysticism those who become sacrifices to the passion of love destroy their lives forever, as the dying moth surrenders to the singeing flame, leaving nothing but ashes. It is quite different in Christ. In his flame, no loving believer shall perish in silence. In Christ, the weaker life is not meant to lose itself in the stronger. The stronger has no wish to overpower the weaker and swallow it up. Christ kills the old in order to give life to the new. Self-will, which is sick unto death, must die. A renewed and transformed will shall come to life. The old will, already turned toward death, falls prey to it. The new will becomes free – to belong to the other life. It is roused in order to live. In God it is given strength to serve this life in deed and in truth.

2 Cor. 5:17

God's will is for our resurrection so that we can live to the full extent of our powers. Basic to the new life is its voluntary nature. Resurrection from death leads to a life of freedom. When this becomes a reality, it means that the greatest of tasks has been effectively assigned. Those who proclaim judgment and death without this commission of life turn God into a judge pronouncing the death sentence or into a

John 8:31–36

cold, indifferent stranger. They have denied the living God. The life-giving Spirit of Jesus Christ does not allow himself to be relegated to a distance. In him, superabundant life, with all its powers of renewal through love, remains concentrated on the earth and its inhabitants. God's creative power, calling forth new life, draws near to all who want the life that is in God. This life is the worldwide rule of God.

Acts 17:26–28

The life-creating Spirit blows where he wills. He comes as he wills. He knows where he wants to go. Everywhere, he seeks out anyone with a determined faith who accepts no other spirit than this one and only Spirit of Life. To such he reveals himself as a power that breaks in across all distances. He proves himself as almighty power; our strength, in comparison, is nothing. It is not we who awaken him; he awakens us.

John 3:8

2 Cor. 4:7

1 Cor. 2:4–5

In the face of his direct breaking-in, all human delusions must give way, vanquished by ultimate reality. Truth dispels all illusions. The sick and misguided spiritual life is cast aside. The self-serving psychophysical life, perishing without light or warmth, is overpowered. Selfish life, in and of itself already condemned to death, is destroyed in the consuming fire of God's approach. Severed from the divine core of life, it was lost before it was abolished.

1 Cor. 3:11–15

Rom. 8:6

Even though it had died long ago, the life of the individual in its own nature was still wrongly called life. The madness that makes an individual think in deathly stupor that he or she is "the only one" must be shattered. In morbid presumption, individuals who think they are "the only one" claim as their property what belongs to God. This self-conceit must die. The other life, God's life, has to begin, in which individuals are freed from their own life and won for the greatness and power of God – received into the sphere of God's power. What was dead wins community with life.

Inner rebirth brings outward change

Here, in this personal contact with God's life, an existence begins that encompasses everything. It cannot become sick and cannot pass away. The life that has its source in God puts its boundless energy to work in a practical way: all its members and powers come to life in the service of justice and righteousness. Then we are received into the sphere of God's kingdom. The nature of this kingdom is the rule of love. God's life is love. Divine love, which wants justice and righteousness first and foremost, brings forth in believers a social and moral life of perfect love. Those set free in this way experience a transformation: they come nearer and nearer to the perfect image of love's radiant power, the reflection of the Lord and Creator of life alone.

Rom. 6:19

1 Col. 1:12–13

Such an experience of God brings about a new birth that lifts us high above all deadening enslavement. This rebirth is the gateway into the kingdom of God. From a new relationship with God, an absolutely new energy and joy in life begins. The beginning of life is birth: new life begins with rebirth. Only in God can life, real life, life in its fullest sense begin. Life is free to unfold only where God has absolute rule. God is life. Because Jesus was one with God, he could and had to say, "I am the life." Because he fills us with his life, the fountainhead of strength, he had to say, "He that believes in me has life."

John 11:25

John 3:15–16

We are able to and should live his life because he
sends his Spirit into our hearts and he himself, with
the Father, makes his dwelling in us. Through his   John 14:23
strength, we keep his word and do the deeds of his
love. Whoever claims that he abides in him is duty-
bound to live as he lived. Because he brought God to   1 John 2:6
us as working and unhampered life, Jesus alone can
satisfy the hunger and thirst for living righteousness.
Only Jesus, in his human existence, has put into
action the vital energy that comes from perfect love.
Only he can reveal God to us as life. Only Jesus, who
is one with the Father and made the life of love a
historical reality on earth, can disclose to us human
beings the mystery and the power of life.

Through the power of the indwelling Spirit of God,
by which Jesus drove out all other spirits, the rule
of God has come to us. Through the life of Jesus, we
shall know what it means to belong to the kingdom
of God. How dare we speak of this kingdom if we
are not prepared to live here and now, in deed and
in truth, as Jesus lived, to place here and now all
circumstances of our life under God's rule? When
we pray for God's kingdom to come, we ought to stop
and ask ourselves whether we are prepared, whether
we want to accept and represent all the changes that   Matt. 6:9–10
God's rule involves.

Jesus shows us that the kingdom of God means
recognizing the absolute supremacy of the highest
will, the will to love. The final kingdom is the perfect
realization of the will of God, who is life and love.
The unconditional nature of God's life and God's love
will not let itself be restricted. God's will does not
allow any other will to stand. The rule of love will not
ally itself with anything that curtails love, restricts

it, or limits it. God's rule will not tolerate any rival authority. The kingdom of God is power because it is the righteousness of God, the peace of Jesus Christ, and joy in the Holy Spirit.

Rom. 14:17

For our day and age, God's rule can already begin in hearts where he and his peace reign because Christ has made his dwelling there. God has sent the Spirit of his Son into human hearts. That carries an obligation and an authority with it – all those gripped by this Spirit must drive all other spirits from every sphere of their life. The kingdom of God has power to make its spiritual laws valid, also for the outward form of human life. The righteousness valid in God's eyes rules so effectively through the Holy Spirit that it can build up social justice – spoken about by the prophets – in the entire surroundings of those who let their lives be governed by it. All spirits of human privilege and social injustice are cast out by the Holy Spirit.

Gal. 4:6

Peace ruling in people's hearts as God's unity enables them to become builders and bearers of outward peace. From the church of God as the center, the driving-out of all spirits of unpeace, war, and civil war, including the spirit of competition and private property, will take place. Joy in the love of God fills the believing heart with such overflowing joy that it must go out to all people in love. As recipients of this faith and joy, one after another shall be drawn into the circle of love and complete community. The spirit of the church is the spirit of justice, peace, and joy, for it is the spirit of the kingdom. It is the church of Jesus Christ that brings the kingdom of God down to earth here and now.

Eph. 2:20–22

The Spirit of God is a power working within our hearts, but this has outward consequences. The effect on society is to break off all existing relationships and build them up completely new. Whoever denies this betrays the innermost nature of this power, for the Spirit of Unity wants community in all things. He achieves unity among us because he brings us into unity with God. The oneness he brings about expresses itself in our lives in such a way that all the evil and unrighteousness in us is overcome through the goodness and love of God.

Eph. 4:3–4

To every situation, such a spirit brings a superior power that is in God alone; it can never originate with people. The will of faith strengthens life for a flood of activity. This faith is the confident trust that radiates from hearts gripped by God. Love is poured out into a believing heart. This takes place through the Spirit, through the living and objective Spirit, who brings with him God's life and God's cause. Faith is something so clear and definite in content – in a personal way and in an objective way – that it cannot be separated either from the believing heart or from the object of faith. Christ himself is this faith, so that Paul declared: "I live, yet not I but Christ lives in me. For the life I live now in the flesh I live by faith in the Son of God, who loved me."

Rom. 5:5

Gal. 2:20

We are saved by grace

There is no other life of faith than that lived in the unity and community in which Christ lives. Faith lives in Christ. Before life can be restored and renewed, there must be an innermost relationship of unity; the believer is in Christ, and Christ is in

him – that is the power that transforms the whole
of life from within. Martin Luther[3] expressed this
mutual relationship between Christ and the individual heart in the most challenging way. He went
through years of struggle, striving in vain after the
righteousness of God with all kinds of human efforts;
for this reason, his experience of God has such an
unprecedented historical importance. The consciousness of sin that characterized him had thrown him
into agony before the face of God, an agony so great
and so severe that many cannot understand it today.
Anyone who has lost the feeling of terror before God's
might will never be able to understand this agony.
And those who do not know Luther's distress can also
not grasp his faith.

God seemed so full of wrath to Luther that he
did not know which way to turn. He could find no
consolation, either from within or from without. His
agony of soul rose to such a pitch that it was infernal:
no tongue could express it, no pen describe it. He
felt he must perish utterly; he had to admit it. God's
greatness and might threw him to the ground. Fear
before God's justice crushed him. Only through the
experience of love could help come to him. He experienced it in the righteousness that springs from grace.
Rom. 3:24   Luther understood "justification" (a word grown
alien to us) to mean the experience of God whereby,
through Christ, faith makes us "good" without our
own efforts or works. Without this we cannot live
Rom. 12:1–2   before God, before ourselves, or before others.

The new element that put Luther's heart and
life on a completely different foundation was the

---

3 Martin Luther, 1483–1546, key figure in the Protestant Reformation.

relationship of mutual exchange between him and
Christ. He expressed it very briefly and to the point
in a letter to his friend Georg Spenlein:

> Learn to know Christ, and him crucified. Learn to
> sing his praises and in your despair about yourself to
> say to him: "You, Lord Jesus, are my righteousness,
> but I am your sin. You have taken upon yourself what
> was mine and given me what was yours; you have
> accepted what you have not been and given me what
> I have not been." . . . Learn from Christ himself how
> in accepting you he has made your sins his and his
> righteousness yours.[4]

1 Cor. 2:2

This mutual relationship, this receiving and giving
of one to the other, is Luther's understanding of
the words: "I live, yet not I but Christ lives in me."
He understands with this confession that the bond
between the believer and Christ is so complete that it
is impossible to separate faith from Christ. Luther is
convinced that in faith one can say with confidence:
"I am Christ – everything he has is mine." This certainty of being one with Christ is based on Christ's
surrender to us. Brought about by Christ, it lives in
our surrender to him. Faith gives us everything we
are and have. When this surrender takes place, it
becomes the strongest willpower that can be brought
into being in us. Our own will is never capable of it.
To say about myself that I no longer live is possible
only when my will has become one with Christ's will
to die. Everything I have ever been or experienced
or achieved must die there where Christ gave up his

Gal. 2:20

1 John 4:19

---

4 Martin Luther to Georg Spenlein, a fellow Augustinian monk, April 8,
   1516.

spirit. Only from Christ's grave is there resurrection of the free will.

The hours in which we come to this experience are hours spent, as it were, in the Black Tower.[5] It is the loneliness of the Crucified One in his death that gives us freedom from our self-importance. It is the step taken by faith, into death and through the grave, that leads to certainty of life: Christ has accepted me in such a real way in his unity with me that he can say, "I am this poor sinner; that is, all his sin and death is my sin and my death." In this unity in death, in spite of the most terrifying consciousness of sin, we become free from all sin. We have life in the Risen One.

What is new in this experience is that we have Christ in us and that he has taken our life upon himself. Our old life is taken away. Through his life, we share all that he is. Everything he possesses will 2 Pet. 1:4 in him be given to us. The same Jesus who said: "All Matt. 28:18 power in heaven and on earth has been given to me" gives us his authority. The same Christ who confesses his unsullied unity with the Father, who takes as his own the seat at the right hand of power, makes us Matt. 26:64 become in him partakers of divinity. Because he has made us his brothers, the Son of Man, who is called the last Adam, has become *our life.* In Christ, the power of him who can give everything to everybody is in us. The throne of all worlds is his. His riches are infinite.

It is often forgotten that Luther recognized as faith the taking hold of the precious and costly treasure itself – that is, Christ. Only Christ himself could give

---

5 Reference to the tower of the Black Cloister in Wittenberg, where Luther experienced his agony and then the saving grace of God.

substance and content to Luther's faith. Only Christ,
"comprehended and dwelling in the heart in faith," is
righteousness. Here is no human definition of faith;   Eph. 3:17
it is simply a matter of Christ. Christ comes down to
us and becomes our life. His coming is faith; what he
does is faith. With all their understanding and good
intentions and church services, the human forces
of piety, wisdom, and religion have no faith. Their
efforts to rise up to God are futile. That I believe in
Christ means that he, Christ, has become one with
me. It means that he abides in me. The life I have in
faith is Christ himself.

This fact that Christ lives in me is what is new
in my life. Where Christ is, the law that condemns
is forever cancelled. Here is Christ, who condemns
sin and throttles death! Where he is, everything that
destroys life must withdraw. "Who shall separate us
from the love of Christ?" Christ is here! No power can   Rom. 8:35–39
sever us from the love of God that is in Christ Jesus
as long as he, the most powerful, is our Master. If I
have lost Christ, there is no help, no consolation, and
no counsel to be had anywhere. The terror of death is
all I know. Life is dead without Christ. Only he is life.
To be with Christ means life and peace within and
without. The life of Christ is energy. God is dynamic
power. Luther says expressly: "A believer has the Holy   John 7:38
Spirit, and the Holy Spirit will not permit a person to
remain idle, but will put him to work and stir him up
to the love of God, to patient suffering in affliction, to
prayer, thanksgiving, to the habit of charity towards
all men."[6] Here we must go beyond Luther, for he goes
no further.

---

6 Martin Luther, *Commentary on the Epistle to the Galatians* (1535).

Christ's justice brings community

Christ living in me means he unfolds his powers in me. Christ wants his power of love to come alive in us with his will to serve and his abundance for giving to others. With all the diversity of his gifts, he wants to be at work in all those who have accepted him as their life. Christ living in us means a wealth of serving and working to be measured only by the need and distress confronting it. When the bowls of wrath are poured out over the world, when misery reaches unbearable heights, then a justice must be proclaimed and put into practice that will be mightier than the injustice over the entire world: all the punitive justice of judgment will be fulfilled in love.

Rev. 16

Through faith, Christ lets the justice and righteousness of God become our justice and righteousness. God's justice cries out to be revealed to all people as the goodness of love. Wherever this justice and righteousness is, anything to do with injustice or selfishness has to withdraw. God's greatness is revealed as the power of love. There is nothing greater than this. When Jesus Christ is the whole content of faith, this faith must be as active in his perfect love as he was. What Jesus accomplished has to be represented by the believer personally and in actual practice. The love born of faith is urged on by the consciousness that the unity of Jesus with the Father was so complete that he said, "What is mine is yours, and what is yours is mine." The unity of faith that binds the human heart to Christ is so completely clear that what Christ says to the believer, the believer also says: "Mine is yours, and yours is mine."

Gen. 15:6
Matt. 5:20

Phil. 2:1–11

John 17:10

Such community of complete sharing must reveal, out of each heart that has experienced it, the same

essential nature and power in all things. A love
that is active on behalf of all sees to it that there is
everywhere a sharing of mine and yours in complete
surrender, bringing everything unitedly to a common
pool for the use of all. Then the believers, as those who
love each other, say to one another, "What is mine
is yours. What is yours is mine." The love of Christ   Acts 2–4
impels them to act and live in this way. The justice
and righteousness of a Christian is Christ and his life.
The Holy Spirit urges toward the same good deeds
that Jesus did. Those gripped by Jesus have, like him,
a love that makes them let go of all privileges. When
they confess that Christ is their life, like Christ they
must choose voluntary poverty for the sake of love;   2 Cor. 5:14
like Christ they must sacrifice their life uncondition-
ally for friends and for foes, with all they are and have.   John 15:13

Jesus was given all power and might. His love,   Matt. 28:18
therefore, must rule unconditionally and unhindered
in the lives of those who are equipped with his
authority. Then from the throne of power he puts his
Spirit into their hearts and gives them his commission.
This commission must fill the whole of life. It must
transform all the circumstances and relationships of
life in accordance with its objective demands.   Matt. 10

We should not say that we believe in Christ and
his kingdom or in unity and community with him if
we do not sacrifice everything and share everything
with one another, just as he did. We should not
claim that his goodness and his righteousness have
become our goodness and our righteousness if we
do not give ourselves to the poor and oppressed just
as he gave everything to them. We cannot think we   Matt. 25:39–40
experience the Strong One, who exercises all author-
ity at the right hand of power, if his works of justice

and community do not come to reality in our lives
through the Holy Spirit. If we have the faith that is
Christ, the working of it must become obvious in
Gal. 5:6   works of perfect love. If Christ rules in us, his rule
must go out from us into all lands. If his Spirit is in
us, streams of this Spirit must transform all the land
around us in accord with his promises about the
coming kingdom.

We need constant spiritual renewal

For such deep-going and far-reaching changes to
take place, we fickle and weak mortals need to be
constantly renewed and deepened – all the more, the
more we are threatened by increasing distractions
and inhibitions. Indeed, at all times our inner experi-
2 Cor. 4:16   ence needs renewal and deepening. Constant renewal
belongs to the realm of the Spirit just as much as to
the natural, physical life. When the sun is shining and
our eyes can see the light, when the birds are singing
and our ears can hear them, it is an actual reality
only because our ears are not deaf, our eyes are not
blind, and our spirit is not dulled. Above all, these
experiences of our mind and spirit can be renewed
only when something actually happens, when God's
mighty power lets the sun rise again every day and
lets the birds begin to sing afresh every year.

1 Pet. 1:23   We are born again through the living Word of God
John 3:1–15   and the blowing Spirit of Jesus Christ. The strength
and power of God does not live in faint recollections.
It is not at work in dead intellectualism. If our spirit
is not to fall prey to death, the Word of Truth, which
creates new life, must prove to be again and again a
James 1:18   living power in our hearts. The Spirit of Life judges

the thoughts and motives of our hearts; he wants to
sever soul from spirit moment by moment so that we
do not become subject to our emotional nature and
unable to perceive the living Spirit.   Heb. 4:12–13

The Spirit of Truth is always ready to fill us anew
and unite us in his church. Christ wants to confer his
power and authority on his church so that through
the Holy Spirit she can time and again win new vic-
tories over all other spirits. It is the work of the Spirit
whenever the Word of God cuts our hearts to the
quick and shows up all confusion in sharp relief. We
need these experiences of the true life-giving Spirit
even more than we need our daily bread.

In the strength of this truth, the Master over all
spirits rejected the encroaching power of the tempter:
"Man shall not live by bread alone but by every word
that proceeds from the mouth of God." If life is not to   Matt. 4:4
die out, we must accept God's truth constantly and
let ourselves be renewed by it. Jesus says therefore:
"My food is to *do* the will of him who sent me." God   John 4:34
lives in deed and action. Our receiving the Word of
God again and again brings forth in us the strength of
God's life and God's deeds from the heart of God.

In this sense, George Fox was right when he began
his great movement in 1647, saying that it was the
Spirit, the inner Light, the inner Word, that was all-
important.[7] The living Word is always waiting to be
received into the innermost ground of our soul – to
be grasped quite personally and so transformed into
actual deeds. This is the only way we can be always
steeled for the hardest battles, as John wrote to his
church communities: "You are strong, the Word of

---

7 George Fox, 1624–1691, founder of the Society of Friends (Quakers).

God abides in you, and you have overcome the evil

1 John 2:14 one." We will abide in the Father and in the Son in all we do only when the direct witness of living truth

John 15:4 abides in us and is constantly renewed.

Every experience of God is undeserved

From the beginning, the Word of God has led us in the atmosphere of grace. Every experience of God is

Eph. 2:8 an undeserved gift. By utterly exposing our incapacity and opposition to him, we have let ourselves be known by God. We have known him in the completely undeserved love he revealed by sacrificing his Son. We have known Jesus as the healing Savior of a life going to utter ruin. Through his death, we have received forgiveness and redemption from the heaviest burdens. Every time we experience God anew, we are led to a deeper consciousness of the deadly interrelationship of all guilt and to a deeper reverence for undeserved grace.

The daily purification of our hearts helps us to see more and more clearly what separates us from God and to take vigorous measures to set it right. God is faithful and just, and when we are ready to take the consequences right to the end, he is prepared to

1 John 1:9 forgive everything that disturbs his unity and purity. When we sin, we need the Advocate, who reconciles

1 John 2:1–2 and unites. Through this Spirit, Christ the mediator wants to set in order all that causes disintegration

Heb. 12:24 and division – all that mars the unity of life. The work of reconciliation blots out guilt and sets free the guilty for life in God – it restores unity.

No one can dispense with the renewal of this experience even for a moment. All the powers of the earth are constantly attacking community with God and the unity of his church. These are in danger of being broken up at any moment. The spirits of mammon, lying, unfaithfulness, and impurity besiege and storm the stronghold of God's community without respite. If we allow them even the smallest foothold in the outer fortress of our being, they concentrate their attack on the very center. Their concentrated fire tries to numb the heart and destroy the unity of life. The soul in our lifeblood is constantly exposed to their destructive rays. As soon as the darkness that surrounds us gains power over our stand in life, we lose community with God. We deliver up the life-blood of our soul to impure powers. We are separated from God and his kingdom by a barrage of dark rays. We are without God and without community in this torn and divided world.

John 3:19

Eph. 5:8–11

Yet the light of unity outshines the darkness of decadence and ruin. We must follow the light. "If we walk in the light as He is in the light, we have fellow-ship with one another, and the blood of Jesus Christ his Son cleanses us from all sin." The bright beams of God's light are stronger than the dark radiation of destructive demonic powers. Light cannot be over-come by darkness, but faith and the life determined by it must be focused steadily on the light. Rays of darkness cannot capture anyone who is turned away from them. Such rays are active in the area of the will and aim at destroying it. If the will keeps free from their poison, the battle is won. The will that lives in the light repels the attacks of darkness. Light is victo-rious over darkness. The will is free.

1 John 1:7

Ps. 139:11–12

John 8:12

Ps. 90:8

Living in community takes living in the light for granted. The life given from God has a clarity and purity that leads to perfect unity of life. It overcomes

all powers of destruction and disintegration. When
we are at one with the soul of Jesus, with his blood
and his life, the purity of his sacrifice sets us free
from all impurity, and the powerful, unifying deed
of his death sets us free from all disunity. This power
brings a life that radiates the same brightness and
glowing warmth as Jesus did and does. The light of
John 12:35–40 Jesus Christ is the new life of perfect unity. Lack of
community and opposition to community are dark-
ness and coldness – turned away from the glowing
light of Jesus. Isolation of soul and impurity of will
are antagonistic to the life of Jesus. The will is impure
and darkened when it mixes the clarity of Jesus' life
with other elements, when it offends the faithfulness
of perfect love or the community of perfect unity, and
when it denies the surrender of all belongings. It for-
sakes the light and chooses darkness when it becomes
selfish, covetous, or possessive. Every disunity and
separation denies the power that radiates from the
sacrificed life of Jesus.

In Christ's death our old life dies

In the spirit of the church, in which Jesus is among
us here and now, he brings about a community that
is united. Only where there is unity is the sacrificial
life of Jesus actively at work. In his church we stand
under the impact of the cross. The cross created our
unity. The Spirit brings it. Without the witness of
the blood of Jesus there is no witness of the Spirit of
Col. 1:20 Christ. Unity is preceded by the abolition of disunity.
The Spirit brings death to the fiend. In the power of
Eph. 1:7 Christ's death our old life dies and new life begins.
Those who lie buried in the churchyard are no longer
to be seen at the tavern, on their property, or carrying

on their own affairs. They have been taken away from the busyness of their old selfish nature.

Those who, with Christ, are dead to all they own turn their backs on all influences of self-will and self-interest. They live in the strength of the sacrificed life of Jesus. In this strength, they sacrifice their own old life just as Jesus sacrificed his perfectly pure life. They are prepared for the same baptism of blood that poured over the body of Jesus. Those who believe in the executed Christ are prepared for death in the strength of an inner dying. If for the sake of truth it has to be, they are even prepared for death with the shame of public condemnation and execution. As a sign of this readiness they are lowered into the grave of Jesus: early Christian baptism is the symbol of the power of dying and the power of resurrection. As a sign of the pouring-out of the Holy Spirit, baptism testifies to the break with things as they are and to the beginning of a new life. Unity in Jesus' death brings unity in God's life. It is only through sacrifice that we can find the courage to enter into the presence of God.

Whoever has experienced God in the holiness of his love, brought close to us by Jesus, knows why Jesus died. God wants us always to be one with the soul of Jesus' blood, dying the death of Jesus, rising in the power of his resurrection, and living the words and life of Jesus. This takes place through the presence of Christ, that is, through the life-giving Spirit, and through Christ's love, poured out over us and filling our hearts. His love draws us into God's community through the Holy Spirit. Dead to everything that is evil and unjust, we live from now on for the good, in the justice and righteousness of perfect love.

2 Cor. 4:11

Matt. 20:22–23

Rom. 6:3–11

Col. 2:12–13

2 Tim. 2:11

God by his very nature can never deprive himself
of his moral character, of his goodness; he can never
enter into community with evil. He cannot end
his own existence. God is the good. He wants to
conquer the world for the good. The good can live
only where evil has died. Our whole nature, which is
shot through and through with evil, has to undergo
the death of Christ as a dying to evil, as our death.
With the Crucified One, we suffer a death that frees
us from all that makes community with God impossible. Delivered up to the judgment of Jesus' death, we
become one with the heart of God in a new life: God
breaks in. What is new begins. What is evil comes to
a stop. What is good starts.

Gal. 2:20

God's heart is revealed in Jesus

The love of Jesus' heart has turned the judgment
of God into redemption. Unity with him who was
executed on the cross brings unity with his soul, with
the very essence of his life. That means unclouded
community with the living God. Community of life
means victory over everything that has anything to
do with sin and death. The death of Christ brings
us to his resurrection. The powers of his sacrificed
life bring us new life from God. This new life proves,
through the working of the Holy Spirit in the resurrection, that Jesus Christ is the living Son of God. In
the Son, the heart of God has come to us. The Spirit
of God brings us his heart. We can perceive his hand
and footsteps in nature and in world history. His
heart is revealed in Jesus. And his heart is mightier
than all his power.

1 John 5:4

John 3:16

Thus the proclamation of the cross becomes a
divine power; coming from the heart of God, it shows

itself as the power for resurrection. Zinzendorf says 1 Cor. 1:17–18
his "rule and method" is "to make the glorious Lamb
everything and to know no blessedness other than
being with him and thanking him and being pleasing
to him."[8] Zinzendorf is talking of the living sacrifice,
which has its joy in the life and work of all-powerful Rom. 12:1–2
love. The Lamb takes the rulership of God's kingdom John 1:29
on his shoulders because he bears the heart of God. If Isa. 9:6
we accept the cross – come life, come death – we take
hold of the risen Christ in the Crucified One. In him,
we believe in the all-victorious power of love, which
is God's heart. The cross is revealed as the victorious
power of perfect love. It leads to resurrection and to
the lordship of God. Jesus Christ, as the revelation
of God's love, is life risen out of death. His death
overcomes all the powers of the world and all deadly
forces. Unless we experience the readiness to die
that characterized his love, we cannot experience his
all-powerful life. Without him, nothing we can do has
the power to withstand death and the devil. Only his
divine life turns our actions into living work. Only
the works of the living God are living. Perfect love as 1 Cor. 13
life that overflows is living work.

We can sense things and experience them, we can
move and be active, only as long as life is at work in
us. There is no way of creating life apart from the
power of life that is God, that is in Christ. When
life flees, our eyes grow blind and our hands droop.
Our ears stop hearing. Our spirit can no longer turn
perceptions into experiences. Our will can no longer
take on any work. In death there is neither strength
nor activity. This power of life – this capacity to take

---

8 Nikolaus Ludwig von Zinzendorf, 1700–1760, leader of the Moravian
Church (Unitas Fratrum).

in experiences – is decisive for being able to act or to create. Only God is life without any death. Only God's vital energy triumphs over death, degeneration, and decay. God rules over all spheres of life as creative life of infinite power.

Jesus cannot be dissected

The wider the circle of our experience, the more active and vital life becomes. The narrower our circle of experience, the more our life becomes stunted. The experience of God encompasses the universality and totality of his almighty works. His creative Spirit is as extensive as it is intensive. Jesus wants to introduce us to the whole of the Almighty's domain. One question is decisive for a life lived in God: whether we want to accept the whole of God or nothing of him, whether we want to accept the whole Christ or only feeble reflections of his image. The faith that God brings

Rev. 3:15–16 into being encompasses the whole, or it is nothing.

Only the whole Christ for the whole of our life transforms and renews everything. Half of Jesus for half of our life is a lie and a delusion. The Spirit of Life tolerates no choosing of principles or elements of faith such as a self-willed spirit selects from God's truth. Truth is indivisible. Christ does not let himself be dissected. Those who do not take the same attitude as Jesus in everything have rejected Jesus. Not even the most ingenious explanation for their halfheartedness protects them from the words: "He

Matt. 12:30 who is not with me is against me."

Those who want to hear, read, or experience one or the other specific thing about Christ yet use weakening interpretations to wipe out what seems impossible

will come to grief no matter how Christian the
edifice of their life seems. Therefore Jesus must say
that all those who hear the words of his Sermon on
the Mount without doing them are like those who
build on shifting sand. Their building is lost from the   Matt. 7:24–27
start. At the first attack of hostile forces, it gives way.

So Jesus commissions his ambassadors: "Teach
them to keep to all I have commanded you." Whoever   Matt. 28:20
loves him keeps his word. Whoever believes in him   John 14:23
does everything he has said. But whoever ignores
even a seemingly small part of his living command-
ments cannot receive Christ's life. Organic unity is
the essence of the Living One. Jesus' life is indivisible.
It withholds itself completely or gives itself completely. It is living unity. Those who want to cut Jesus
into pieces and lay violent hands on his life are left
with nothing but death in their hands.

Christ wants us to experience him as living and
complete, standing in completeness at the center of
living action. His life is integration and wholeness
itself; his life tolerates no mixing with anything
outside its sphere. Thus anything contrary to the
unity of his life and its living task has to give way
before him. True life fights against all ungenuine
life. Where Christ unfolds his divine life, all
other life is extinguished. No other love can exist
beside his perfect love. With divine jealousy, he
annihilates every other image – often a falsified
Christ-image – that we set up beside him.

Over eight hundred years ago, Bernard of Clairvaux said about his experience of this, "When Jesus
comes to me, or rather, when he enters into me,
he comes . . . in love, and he is zealous for me with

divine zeal."[9] The whole Christ wants us wholly. He loves decision. He loves his enemies more than his halfhearted friends. He hates those who falsify him even more than those who are diametrically opposed to him. He abhors what is lukewarm and a colorless gray, the twilight, and the pious talk that blurs and mixes everything and commits itself to nothing. All Matt. 7:21–23 this he sweeps away when he draws near.

Jesus comes to us as he is. He enters into us with his entire word. He reveals himself to our hearts as a coherent whole. In his coming, we experience the full power of his love and the whole force of his life. Everything else is deception and lies. Jesus Christ draws near to no one in a few fleeting impressions. Either he brings the whole kingdom of God forever, or he gives nothing. Only those prepared to receive him completely and forever can experience him. They are given the secret of God's kingdom. To all others Jesus cloaks himself in unrecognizable parables. Whoever holds aloof from complete surrender hears parables Matt. 13:12–14 without understanding them. He has eyes to see and sees nothing. He has ears to hear and understands nothing. Whoever does not want the whole loses the little he thinks he has.

The experience of Jesus Christ is either a confirmation or a delusion. It proves true by holding firmly and with enduring steadfastness to the very beginning, to the whole way, and to the final future of Matt. 24:13 Jesus Christ. So it endures to the end. When Christ is recognized fully, the invincible love of the Spirit overflows with endless insight and knowledge. It fills life

---

9 Bernard of Clairvaux, 1091–1153, in *Sermons on the Song of Songs,* Sermon 69.6.20.

with the fruit of steadfast righteousness, for Christ, the whole Christ, is its righteousness.

The experience of God gives strength

How we conduct our lives proves whether this experience of faith forms the basis of our lives. The Father of Jesus Christ is God the creator. Every experience of God brings power to give life shape and form. Where it comes from God, a form of life takes shape in keeping with the complete picture of Jesus Christ and, therefore, with the kingdom of God. The weaker the life, the less able it is to give life shape and form. The difference between fleeting observations, which skim the surface, and experiences that go deep and remain steadfast can be seen in the power of their effect. Where God is at work, he goes into the depths while he reaches out into the distance. He is power at work giving life shape and form.

How many people travel in rushing vehicles from country to country, hastily skimming over the beauties of the whole world! Their eyes take a quick glance at everything. Yet nothing becomes a lasting experience. Their lives remain infinitely poorer than the lives of many of their neighbors who have never seen anything but the fields or woods outside their hometown, but for whom trees and flowers blossoming and fading or nature stirring in any way becomes a fruitful experience.

Those who go rushing by see nothing in the cities but the deceptive exterior of life. Their less esteemed neighbors, however, know deeply shaking realities in the joy of love, in daily work, and in the need of the world; they penetrate into all that life has to offer

and to the very core of death too. True life is the
all-embracing consciousness that sees deeply into the
essential nature of things and, at the same time, far
and wide into the distance. It bears the suffering of
the world. It hungers after justice and righteousness,
for it has heart and is heart. It is God's heart.

Matt. 5:4–7

In some people, the shattering experiences of
worldwide need, of war, and of all the subsequent
catastrophes have only blunted the conscience.
Others, though, see with new eyes what was previously hidden: the present as it really is and the future
as it truly shall be. The new vision transforms life and
animates every action. Only those who take in fully
the true nature of all things and all events have a true
and enduring experience of life. Truth demands that
the shattering experiences of God's *wrath* sweeping
over the world today and making history touch our
hearts to the quick and change our whole lives. But
truth demands even more strongly that our hearts
and lives are moved by the *love* that appeared in
Christ Jesus as the heart of God.

1 John 4:10–12

No matter how much we may hear and read the
words of Jesus and the story of his life, no matter
how much we say about them according to the letter
of the Bible, lifeless knowledge leads to destruction
if the Spirit and essence of his love does not grip us
and our whole life down to the last detail. The letter
kills. The Spirit gives life. His life is love. If truth, as
the essence of love, does not become all-determining
in our lives, its power kills the conscience. Without
love, the new life dies before it is born. Truth also has
a deadly effect when its life-giving works are rejected.
Whoever hardens his heart to the transforming
power of its living nature will be killed by truth.

2 Cor. 3:6

The effects of an experience show whether it has
been significant or empty, whether it has awakened
life or killed it. Every experience of the unfalsified   Matt 7:16
Christ brings energy that proves itself in actual life.
The renewal of our mind and nature brings about
a transformation. In this transformation we give
up ourselves, and all we have, to serve God and
his kingdom alone. The results prove whether we
have experienced God or whether we have become
entangled in the veil of maya.[10] For God has a power   Gal. 5:22
of life and love that his creatures are never capable
of. The experience of God brings a superhuman love
because it brings God's life. Love pours itself into the
heart. The Holy Spirit transmits the divine power of
this love.

The experience of God means strength for action.
There is no love that does not come to living expression in deeds. To experience God as a life of love is
to experience strength. A freeing from all unjust,
loveless, and self-willed activity liberates abundant
powers, which then achieve fruitful works of love.
The love of God is experienced in the innermost
heart and unfolds toward the outside. The more faith
increases in knowledge, experience, and strength, the
more must we do the works of love. To experience   Eph. 4:13
God is to be overwhelmed by the power of love.

The world situation today calls for the kind of
dedication that lives in Christ alone, in the heart of
the powerful God of Jesus Christ. Only a heart filled
with the superior power of God's love will be able
to check need and distress and alleviate suffering.
Only in the strength of the omnipotent God can

---

10 A concept in Hindu philosophy often translated as "illusion."

we carry the burden of historical responsibility laid on us today, a burden beyond all human strength. The perfect strength of all-powerful love, surpassing every other power or greatness, is needed to penetrate our devastated world with God's rule and Christ's message.

In the midst of the escalating power of injustice, in the midst of today's widespread cruelty and coldness of heart, love must be revealed: a love that towers above all the mountains of earth; that shines out more clearly and brightly than all the stars of heaven; that is more powerful and mighty than the quaking of the earth and the eruption of all its volcanoes; that is greater than all world powers and ruling authorities; that works more powerfully on history than all catastrophes, wars, and revolutions; that is more alive than all life of the creation and its most powerful forces. Above all nature and throughout all history, love proves itself as the ultimate power of the Almighty, as the ultimate greatness of his heart, as the ultimate revelation of his Spirit.

1 Cor. 13:13

The experience of God is love – love that overcomes everything that withstands it. Love is the energy of the new creation. It is the Spirit of God's coming rule. Love is the one and only element in the new building-up. It is the herald of a new time. It is the organic strength of unity. It is the building-up of a new humankind. This love is put into practice by the unity found in the church of Jesus Christ. The building-up of the church means a gathering. Whoever does not gather with her scatters. Her life consists in uniting. Whoever does not take part in this uniting remains in death. In the midst of an age

1 John 4:8

Eph. 2:14–22

of decline, the life-bringing Spirit of Jesus Christ establishes the work of the church. In her, God is experienced in Christ. In the church of perfect love, the Spirit of God brings Christ's kingdom of perfect justice and righteousness down to the earth. The experience of God means the reign of God in the church of Jesus Christ.

The Peace of God

Peace is unity and justice

A deep-seated human need makes us long that the whole of life be included in a universal harmony. Our inmost feeling tells us that the life ordained by God is one of organic unity, unity of all powers of the spirit and the will. In actual experience, however, the fate of unpeaceful humankind today is petty limitation, discord and disunion, inorganic confusion, and conflict of spirits and aims. We have no unified center, no living point from which our entire thinking and doing can radiate. We lack this common point of reference, from which any effective unity must be determined if life is to prove itself strong and undivided. This dynamic integrity of life has been lost to individuals and to humankind.

Only where peace is alive and active and where its harmonious working embraces the whole of life can a clear conscience acknowledge peace. There can be no talk of peace or harmony if a life does not show its integrity in lively activity and rich diversity. Impassive silence and unbroken quiet belong only to the deathly peace of the graveyard. Life is energy for enthusiastic action and reality in all its facets. Where the life-giving Spirit of God's peace fills and unites us, he puts his infinite energy into deeds of love that are varied yet consistent, animated yet stable, diverse yet whole and undivided. The peace of God is the dynamic harmony of the perfect life, vibrant with infinite riches. "Whoever finds me, finds life" is the revelation it brings.

1 John 4:12
1 John 5:12
Prov. 8:35

God's life is love. That is why he is the God of peace. His will is unity. In Jesus Christ, the revelation of God's ultimate will, the supreme power of the Almighty brings a peace the world cannot offer. Jesus brings God's peace to us. In Jesus, God's countenance is so illuminated that it brings an inmost peace of heart, a national peace that is justice, and an end to all warfare through love for one's enemies. The peace of God is unity in his creative Spirit, who wants to bring a new peace and unity to the torn state of humankind and the whole world.

John 14:27

Jer. 33:6

When God blesses his people with peace, we must never think exclusively of peace of soul or of a military cease-fire. God's peace brings the new order of a kingdom of peace that carries all before it inwardly and outwardly. God's Prince of Peace makes faithfulness and justice the foundation of the land of peace over which he rules. Under his rulership, justice and peace kiss each other. Where God has been at work, healing and making whole, he grants perfect peace on the stable basis of constancy and faithfulness of heart and mind and manner of life to the very end.

Ps. 85:10

Whoever obeys his Spirit says with the prophets: "As
long as I live, peace and faithfulness shall reign." Isa. 39:8

God creates peace on the basis of a justice that by
its very nature can serve nothing but peace. The Lord Isa. 32:17–18
of peace consecrates every aspect of human life to his
perfect purity and unity. He demands the surrender
of all the goods of this life and of life itself. His new
justice gives the poor and the wretched the land they
never had; great peace shall be their joy. Without Ps. 37:11
justice there is no peace. If the land of this stolen
earth is not given back to the poor, justice will remain
lost. For the poor who have been robbed of land,
justice demands that everything amassed in self-will
and opposition to God's will is handed back again.
God's justice overcomes self-will and private property. What people own hinders God's unity. With the
doing of good deeds, the peace of God supplants the
evil of discord and strife.

Peace belongs to all who do good by giving up
everything to love. It belongs to them alone. It
streams out from the mercy of God and reveals his
heart. Where his peace rules is good in abundance. James 3:18
The world peace of Christ establishes the order of
love and justice for all people and for all things. The
peace of God, as the future of God's kingdom, is to
have complete sovereignty over world affairs as well
as over local churches. This takes place through
the unity of the church of Jesus Christ, through the
united nature of the innermost life. In the church of
Jesus Christ, the peace of God reveals the infinite
power and united nature of God's heart. His all-
conquering supremacy shall penetrate and master all
things and all beings to unite them in God.

God's peace lasts forever

When God says, "Peace be with you," and the Risen

John 20:19, 21, 26

One gives his "peace" to his disciples, when the early Christians and all the powerful Christ-movements of the Middle Ages and Reformation greet each other with "Peace," we must acknowledge the joyful certainty and the power in this blessing of God's unity. The peace of God brings the grace of Jesus Christ and the power of the Holy Spirit. It encompasses the complete supremacy of God's rule, which as the unity of the creative Spirit aims at bringing all created things into God's unity. Whoever believes in the all-surpassing power of God is full of courage and confidence that his peace will be victorious. Faith in

1 John 5:4

the peace of God is courage in a heart sure of victory.

Peace stands in opposition to fear. Peace, as unity springing from life in God, overcomes the fear of

Heb. 2:14–15

dissolution in death. The greeting of peace to Gideon was to encourage him to live: "Fear not, you shall not

Judg. 6:23

die!" Unpeace belongs to the kingdom of death. Peace allows life to triumph over death. Unpeace bears within it the fear of death. Peace is freedom for a courageous life of justice and righteousness. Unpeace is slavery to injustice and to the fear of death that arises from it. People justify preparations for war on the grounds of security measures, because they are anxious in the face of oppression and danger. They fear injustice and the loss of freedom. Yet these very preparations bring nothing but injustice and slavery. The unpeace in the individual's struggle for existence also stems from weakness and fear and results in

Matt. 6:25–34

nothing but unfreedom and injustice. Those who fear do not have perfect love.

Fear for our own lives prevents us from keeping peace and doing works of righteousness and justice. When the power of love overcomes enervating fear, the strength of abiding peace enters. It builds up everlasting justice. "There is no fear in love, but perfect love casts out fear." An armistice with armies lying in readiness, fearing renewed hostilities, cannot be called peace. An armed peace is no true peace. Only the rule of peace that will last for ever and ever, as promised to the House of David, is true peace. Only eternal peace is true peace.

1 John 4:18

God alone rules over eternity. Man does not even reign over the very small span of time allotted to him. There is no peace other than God's peace. Peace treaties and great congresses and conferences among nations have spoken about everlasting peace. They know temporary peace is meaningless. Yet they cannot achieve peace. A significant work written by Immanuel Kant in 1795, looking back from his mature old age, bears the characteristic title *To Eternal Peace.* A hundred years earlier, the Quaker William Penn had also demanded peace for Europe for both the present and the future.[1] Both point to the divine character of peace. Only perfect life has no end. To us mortals and our undertakings only a brief span is allotted. Only God's peace and the kingdom of the Prince of Peace, who is arisen from the dead, have no end. Human works must retreat before God's works: "When he rules far and wide, peace will have no end."

Jer. 6:14
Ezek. 13:10–16

1 John 2:17
Isa. 9:7

Lasting peace can only be guaranteed from above, from that which is eternal and immortal. It can never be established by time-bound powers. Only the

---

1 William Penn, 1644–1718, "An Essay towards the Present and Future Peace of Europe," 1693.

infinite power of God can build up unity and preserve peace. Everything mortal falls prey to dissolution and decomposition. Life has to overcome death if unity of life is to be won and kept. When scripture says God will bless his people with peace, it as much as promises he will give the strength of his eternal and unchangeable power. God is life. God is strength. In the strength of his life, he is the God of peace.

1 Cor. 15:53–55

Ps. 29:11

Peace is constructive work

God is the creative force that brings about and creates a life that builds up unity. His joy in peace delights in energetic action and demands active mutual help; he wills into being a community of work that creates things of value. The peace of God is grounded in creative justice. Peace is God's work. There is no peace in creation without the Creator, just as there is no outward peace without the inner peace of social justice and no justice without community of creative work. God alone is love. Peace is created only when his spirit of love is at work.

Eph. 4:1–6

If we do not use all means and God-given powers to pass on to the poor and downtrodden all the goods and strength we receive from God, we should not talk of peace. Peace is helping one another through deeds done in love to God. Unless this power is at work, everything stays lifeless, nothing is at peace. Talk about establishing outward peace is false prophecy from those who do not build up active peace through loving work in community. What they call peace cannot be peace. The object of peace is missing: the building-up of unity through mutual help.

1 Thess. 5:3

When foreign ambassadors came to David, the king of Israel, and spoke of peace, he said to them,

"If you come to me peaceably to help me, my heart shall be knit to yours." Only mutual help and service in action is living peace. The lifeless peace that is all negation, such as the abolition of war, the peace that is satisfied when people lay down arms and stop killing, is an empty nothing. The same is true when people claim they have peace in their hearts simply because the fire of inner conflict has died down. 1 Chron. 12:17–18
Rom. 14:18–19

The peace of God brings the strength of God's life. It brings the power of his love. It is active deed and service. To the first challenge "Lay down your arms!" belongs the second "Pick up your tools!" Depart from evil and do good! Turn your back on war, and with all your strength build up the communal work of peace. Peace is constructive work. Isa. 2:4
Ps. 34:14

Peace is born when justice comes to the light of day as a living body. The church of Jesus Christ is this body, this organism of justice, peace, and joy in the Spirit. This is why the Psalmist says both things: "The mountains shall bring peace, and the hills shall bear justice! At the given time, justice and righteousness shall arise for you. With the rising of the sun of justice, the day of great peace dawns." This day has dawned in Jesus. In Christ, it draws near anew. When justice shines forth, peace is guaranteed. Ps. 72:3
Ps. 37:6

The land must be opened up to love. Starting from thinking and believing hearts, peace is making its conquest of the earth today through the church. If peace is to reign within city walls, true counseling of justice must be found for everyone and put into practice. The city that is the church of God is responsible for carrying out this counsel of peace. Whoever wants God's peace has to think the thoughts of peace, God's thoughts. The church, in thinking the thoughts Ps. 122:6–9 of Jesus, is the bearer of God's heart. Hearts thinking the truth of Jesus know in love what counsel to give, and do what needs to be done. Where God is at work, faith is present. Faith is action. Faith produces love. Love knows what to counsel. When Jesus commands

Mark 9:50 us to have the biting salt of truth, he is referring to the peace that the believers have among themselves and take out into the world.

God's truth brings peace

Truth ends the disorder of unpeace so the order of peace can arise. The God of peace and order wants to stop the inorganic scattering of our thoughts and end the disorder of all things in our world that obstruct peace. Without Jesus Christ, people cannot find the

Mic. 4:12 way of peace because they do not recognize it. And they do not recognize it because their thoughts are

Isa. 59:7–8 bent on the divergent ways of unpeace. They are unclear about the main condition for true peace and

Rom. 3:9–18 just as unclear about its needed consequences.

If we are to recognize and avoid all other ways as divergent and leading to destruction, if we are to set foot on the way of peace and go with peace in our hands to those without it, then the spirit of wisdom

1 Cor. 14:33 must reveal the whole truth hidden in God's unity. Our hearts must become rigorously honest in the light of truth if we are to live up to the wisdom that comes from peace. The peace of God is given through

Prov. 2:7 the truth – but only to the upright. "Seek what is
Ps. 37:37 upright and you shall have peace."

Only to the upright is wisdom given; only wisdom opens up the way of peace. When God speaks about peace, he speaks against unpeace as folly. The practical wisdom of God seeks peace. Jealousy and strife are marks of folly, of worldly, emotional, and devilish wisdom that brings nothing but evil and disorder with it. Wisdom from God brings peace, for it is full of mercy and good deeds. Directed toward all people without any hypocrisy or partiality, God's wisdom is all-embracing. As long as we remain pettyminded and aloof from the oneness of the whole and put what is isolated and individual in the limelight, we remain torn by untruthfulness and sunk in confusion. We are not at peace but get lost in superficialities, persist in folly, and remain in death.

James 3:15–18

Some want to talk exclusively about the peace of their own soul or the peace they share with another. They are incapable of representing the whole peace of God that belongs to the final kingdom. They remain sunk in narrow-minded folly, bogged down in the swamp of isolation. But it is the same with those friends of peace who make the opposite mistake and speak about world peace without peace with God and without the social justice of complete community. They want "pacifism" without fighting the spirits of unpeace, without battling the covetous nature of mammon, without opposing the accepted lies of social insincerity, and without waging spiritual warfare against unfaithfulness and impurity. Both of these false paths in life represent unpeace that comes from folly and indifference to all-embracing truth.

Wisd. of Sol. 14:22

In wisdom and faithfulness, peace is a reality. The kingdom of God is the union of love and truth. Therefore to unite outward peace with inner righteousness is the whole will of God's love. Only hearts that love the whole truth have peace, and only such

people bring peace and work for it. God's truth brings
wisdom and uprightness – it begets perfect love. Love
is the ultimate truth – it brings peace.

2 John 1–6

1 Cor. 13:6–7

We keep peace only when the truth of God is in
our hearts and our lives are upright in accordance
with his perfect love. Only this truth in love and this
love in truth makes for peace. When we do what God
lays upon us, we shall – in the truth of love – bring salt
and strength, help and loving-kindness to all people.
In this love born of truth, peace is guaranteed by
loving-kindness and faithfulness.

Ps. 25:10

Peace frees us to serve

Out of thoughts of what is good, peace is born. In the
strength of peace, we want what is good for all people
and all things. A heart that thinks evil cheats itself
and everyone else: it becomes unhappy and spreads
unhappiness. But whoever works for peace through
the good – only love born of truth is good – brings the
joy of life to people. Everything that offends love – the
love that is the truth of God and his universe – is evil.
Whoever represents the good for all with the unfail-
ing power of perfect love puts into practice the peace
of God, which is the ultimate truth of God's decrees.

Matt. 12:33–35

Rom. 13:8–10

The Prince of Peace is also called the Wonderful
Counselor, the Mighty God, and the Everlasting
Father. The kingdom that rests on the shoulders of
the Son of Man is one of peace because it has the
counsel of wisdom, the strength of might, and the
divinity of the Father of Jesus Christ. The Creator
of the new creation establishes the divine work of
eternal peace: God's counsel leads to peace as the
kingdom over which he rules.

Isa. 9:6–7

Plough Quarterly

FREE TRIAL ISSUE

Thank you for your purchase. If you liked this book, you'll want to try our magazine as well. Plough Quarterly brings together a diverse community of readers serious about putting their faith into action. And since you bought one of our books, we'd like to offer one issue free.

Give it a try! Just drop this completed card in the mail, and we'll send you a free trial issue. No cost, no obligation. If you like it, you'll get four more issues for just $18 (£14, €16). If you decide not to subscribe, simply write "cancel" on the invoice, return it, and owe nothing. Either way, the trial issue is yours to keep.

Please allow 4–6 weeks for delivery of your free issue. No need to send money now; we will bill you later.

Plough Quarterly is $40 per year by single copy, so you save 55%.

www.plough.com/trial

Name

Address

City   State   Zip

Email (We will not share your email address with any third party)

B2OBK

The quiet and security of God's household of peace makes us free to dedicate ourselves to the task. Hands freed from defense should be active in building up the city of God. When the pickax is not used as a weapon, it serves as a tool. Limbs not warring on the side of injustice work for justice. Only then do we become true men and women. The faithfulness shown in dedicated work is God's peace in practical community. `Eph. 4:28`

The peace of God works like a stream, a wind; it is almighty power. Only God's peace can move all the mills of human activity, like a mighty river whose waters overflow, whose depths and force produce the greatest achievements. Whoever wants well-being of the people, building-up of the city, productive employment instead of demoralizing unemployment, and the healing of human society must want peace as God wants it. As work in community, in a completely united society, peace is the only state that brings inner and outer well-being. `Isa. 48:18` `Isa. 54:10–17`

Love as God's peace is the bond of perfection that unites everything that was split apart and leads it to complete surrender and common action. The Lord of peace wants to establish and maintain unity – in infinite diversity – for all things, however dissimilar. Peacemakers must represent God's peace as the solution for all problems, however remote. God's inmost nature manifests a power that overcomes everything. It overlooks and neglects nothing but is concerned with everything. God's heart is the mightiest power of all superterrestrial worlds, of all the powers of eternity. The peace of God's heart shall "have dominion from sea to sea, from the River to the ends of the earth." `Col. 1:19–20` `Ps. 72:8`

Peace calls for warriors

Eph. 2:17

Jesus proclaims peace to all, far and near, as part of the fighting equipment of his mission. The feet of his

Eph. 6:10–17

ambassadors must be shod with it for carrying his truth on long journeys into all lands. The message of peace as a fighting commission shall conquer all countries for God's rule with weapons of the Spirit. Only for this task will the Lord and Commander of peace be on our side. Just as Jesus sacrificed his life in the decisive battle to establish peace, so we too should be ready to lay down our lives. Whoever is not ready to fall in battle for the truth cannot live for peace.

When Jesus gave his ambassadors the commission to proclaim God's coming reign, he wanted peace and its powerful effect announced to each house open to them. Their peace descended in God's full truth on each house they visited. If a house was not ready and willing, the peace, like a boomerang, would return to

Matt. 10:11–14

the hands of the warrior of peace. Peace is the salting

Mark 9:49

power of fire, the spiritual weapon of the kingdom of God, the sword of the Spirit.

Peace is the flaming eye of the armies of God. It is the battle song of his heavenly hosts: "Glory to God in

Luke 2:13–14

the highest! Peace on earth to men of good will!" In the strength of this peace the Messiah-King entered the walls of Jerusalem. He rode no warhorse to a battle in which blood would be shed. The animal of poverty and peace was carrying him when he heard the cry, "Hail to him who comes in the name of the

Luke 19:28–38

Lord! With him is peace!" Defenseless, he rode to meet his death. Victorious, he sacrificed his life to lay the foundation of peace, carrying into all the world a bloodless battle against the power of the bloody sword, a battle for the complete dominion of the

Spirit. Whoever glimpses the King of Peace enters his kingdom in unsullied peace even though, like him, he must ford the terrifying river of death.

God's peace is the Spirit's victorious and death-defying battle against the evil spirit of devilish unpeace. In his defenseless death, Jesus destroyed the deadly weapons of the enemy just as the God of peace will soon crush Satan under the feet of the Spirit. He establishes peace in an all-out battle to the point of dying a defenseless death. He does not bring that flabby lack of hostilities people call peace. He brings the sharp sword of spiritual warfare, but those in his Spirit sacrifice their lives without killing their enemies.

Rom. 16:20

Heb. 4:12–13

Jesus went to his death to bring peace. He killed no one, but he was killed. Without defending or sparing his life, he let his body be broken on the tree, welding hostile nations into one united people of peace, one single and united humankind. In the death struggle of his body, he gave humankind a new body: his living, united organism of peace – the church of Jesus Christ.

Eph. 2:14–22

Anyone who wants to belong to this new, united body must be ready like Jesus to suffer the most shameful and cruel death, to accept the same cup of poison from enemy hands, to be baptized by the enemy in the same bloodbath of the death sentence. Anyone who wants to live for the peace of God has, without sparing his or her own life, to take on the same fight to the death that Jesus fought to the end for the kingdom of peace. This is why the human heart is terrified and shakes with fear when the Risen One stands before it with the marks of death upon him to pass on his peace and his trenchant mission.

Matt. 20:22–23

1 Pet. 2:19–25

The militant peace of Jesus Christ is unknown to humankind. The world knows only hate with its murderous preparation for war or the insincere and uncreative flabbiness of peace without struggle and without unity. The world knows only blind rage leading to the mass murder of war or the untruth of false prophecy that spares the individual's own life but cannot represent an effective peace.

Isa. 59:7–8

Because humanity does not wish to know the ways of sacrifice that lead to peace, it lacks those concrete and detailed thoughts that flow from God's will to unity. Peace blooms on the soil of genuine truthfulness that is shown only in a life sacrificed to the utmost and spent in unarmed but out-and-out combat against all opposition to unity and constructive peace. The heart that makes the perfect sacrifice – the mightiest power of all worlds – is the only strength that can bring peace.

Rom. 12

Peace demands purity

Love fighting for unity makes this perfect sacrifice, which demands inmost purity of heart so that our whole life might be pure. Because Jesus poured out the soul of a pure life in his sacrificial death and commended an unstained spirit of divine love into the hands of the Father, he triumphed as the pure one over the prince of death and his impure spirits. Purity atones and must rise again. Impurity not atoned for leads to death and remains in death. Not even by sacrificing its life can an impure life gain peace. Unity demands purity.

Heb. 9:11–15
Phil. 4:8–9

Heb. 12:14–16

The unbridled passions of youth bring the deadly unpeace of impure spirits. These passions undermine trust and destroy faithfulness. They break up the

coherence of life. Peace born of living unity exists
only in the pure air of trust and faithfulness. Purity,
trust, and faithfulness make up the atmosphere of
life and of all viable community. Those who want to   2 Tim. 2:22
devote their strength to a living peace must strive for
the sanctification of dedicating their whole lives to
God's pure cause.

In the long-suffering humility of Jesus Christ's
sacrifice lies hidden the purity of a life dedicated to
God's unity. It wishes to take command of our lives
in the pure Spirit of Jesus. God's peace is unmerited
grace. Only through a direct gift of God is our life at
any moment pure and blameless in the absolute peace
of God's heart. All the gifts of his Spirit are gifts of
peace, to be used in the service of the pure unity of   1 Cor. 1:10–13
his church.

Christ's ambassadors proclaim peace

The house of God upholds peace and tolerates no
breach, no irritation and strife within or hate and
enmity to those without. All unpeace is banned from
this house. Here dwells joy in all God's gifts, joy in all
the objects of his love. Where God grants his gift of
joyful hearts, born of love that includes everybody, his
peace gathers a people in creative unity. God brings
about a righteousness of faith that grants peace with
God, which is his will for all people. The Holy Spirit   Isa. 32:16–18
who fills the church of faith means life in God, peace
with God, and peace for all people. The fruit of this
Spirit is love and peace, the joy of a life in God.   Gal. 5:22

Peace is the daughter of faith. Like faith, it surpasses all human understanding. As an offspring of
the Spirit of Jesus Christ, peace keeps the heart and
mind in him. Unity born of the Spirit of God can   Phil. 4:7

accomplish what the thoughts and demands of the understanding never can. Faith conceives this unity, just as Mary conceived. Now as then, it is the body of Jesus Christ that is born; the united church is born of God's creative Spirit through faith. She surpasses everything that is human. Starting with the hearts of believers, she has power to rule and direct them; and she brings peace into all the world. Like the birth of Christ, every commission to the church of God is given in peace and unity. Her ways are ways of peace, just as the ways of Jesus Christ were, are, and always will be peace among all nations. Therefore the sons and daughters of God delight in creating and in

Matt. 5:9 bringing peace alone. The kingdom of God belongs to peace.

God himself is in his sons and daughters, for they carry his blessing as peacemakers, carry out God's commands, live to give him joy, and do their utmost to keep peace with everyone. Yet they know that peace on earth can only be the fruit of faith in God and Christ and that the godless cannot keep peace, as long as they remain far off from true life. The goal of all Christ said and did, and the goal of his ambassadors, was unity with God and peace among all people

2 Cor. 5:20 as a way of life.

The ambassadors of Jesus Christ proclaim a peace that rules over all areas of their life. They bear the name of the Prince of Peace because Christ is the lord and king of divine peace and holds the universal kingdom of eternal peace in his mighty hand. For them, his kingdom does not exist in sterile words but in the strength and power of the unity that creates

1 Cor. 4:20 the peace of his future world. Sent out from the spirit

of the church where peace rules, they carry its power
into all the world. They fight for the things that serve
peace, making every effort to improve conditions to
help build up the holy peace of God.

For them, peace is the hope of their faith, their
expectation for the future, and a power here and now;
peace is for them the sum total of all God's wisdom
and decrees. God as the Lord, Christ as their expectation, and the Holy Spirit as the power that reveals
all future things fill them with the most confident
joy and inviolable peace. Their peace is not of the
moment, for it comes from him who is, and was, and
is to come.

The prophets foretold this peace

Peace as God's future is proclaimed by the whole
prophecy of the old covenant and the prophetic
mission of the new church. All war and all hostility
are to come to an end. The old prophecy and the new   Isa. 2:2–4
prophecy are one. The prophets of the old covenant   Rev. 21:1–4
and the new covenant bring to bleeding humanity the
divine kingdom of God's peace, which puts an end to
the violent and predatory nature of all ruling powers.
Bestial malice and ferocity will be completely banned.

The predatory nature of brute force is overcome
by the sacrificial nature of long-suffering. The reign   Matt. 5:38–42
of the Lamb replaces espionage and violent killing.   Isa. 53
The sacrificial love of the new man, ready to give
up his own life, takes the place of the old man's life-
destroying injustice and alienation from God – the   Rev. 7:14–17
old man who had forfeited his true human image
from the time of the first Adam and the first fratricide. Humanity will finally become human through

1 Cor. 15:20–22, 45–50 the Son of Man, the last Adam. The heart and soul of the Bible is filled with this certainty. All of divine history in the Bible, and all of human history, leads to this goal.

The book that reveals God in history begins and ends with peace. The inmost depth of the Bible, its life and soul, is and remains peace. Loss of community with God always leads to murderous unpeace. Yet the morning star of the coming peace and unity is never extinguished. After the breach with our origin in the first kingdom of peace, the next step follows immediately – fratricide, which must not be Gen. 4:8–15 avenged. The descendants of the man who murdered his brother proceed to found cities. The fellowship Gen. 11:4–9 of the metropolis – as in the tower of Babel – leads to dire confusion, disintegration, and warlike tensions between nations. Revolt against God leads nations to insurrection and war. Yet God revealed his heart once more: the deluge of his judgment swept over humankind, disunited and resistant to his Spirit; but under the colorful symbol of the rainbow, he established the Gen. 9:13–16 covenant of peace.

The father of faith is consecrated as a prince of peace by a mysterious priestly figure who belongs Heb. 7:1–3 to the united dominion of peace. The faith of the patriarchs turns again and again to peace because the faith of Abraham, Isaac, and Jacob in the one God shows itself as a uniting power. So the greatest blessing of these patriarchs and later of Aaron (the first priest of atonement) is the blessing of peace. Even in the war years of the lawgiver, the blessing of the first high priest culminates in the peace that the last high priest was to turn into reality: "The Lord bless you

and keep you . . . and give you peace!" Through Moses Num. 6:22–27
the Law comes to God's people. In its wake come war
and the sword. The military power of the Israelites
reaches its zenith through the kings given them, at
their demand, by God in his wrath. But despite all
battle songs, at the heart of the psalms of the people
and the songs of the kings there lies a longing for the
peace that shall come from God.

The prophets proclaim peace as justice from God
that shall take possession of the whole world. In the Ps. 72:1–7
midst of the storm of devastating historical events, Isa. 32:17–18
the prophetic message of peace stands like a rock that
cannot be broken. The coming helper and leader of
God's people will calm the raging sea of nations. As
the bringer of peace, Jesus is given the name "Our
Peace." Faced with his strength and truth, every Eph. 2:14
illusion vanishes. The Old Testament prophet sees
the contrast between the conditions of his time and
the divine justice of the coming King of Peace, which
judges and saves. It must shine relentlessly through Isa. 26:1–13
all the evil of the present time; it is love at work, and
its fruit is peace.

When God is involved, so is his creation. Where
God's peace appears, human unpeace is struck at the
root. Social discord is revealed as human injustice
that is enmity to God and an obstacle to peace which
must be identified and ruthlessly exposed. Whoever
sins against people commits an outrage against God. 1 John 4:20–21
The Spirit of Peace demands justice. The divine Spirit Amos 5:8,
in prophecy strikes society at the root of its poisonous 11–15, 24
growth. It exposes economic injustice: hardworking
people shamefully robbed of all meaning in life and Isa. 3:13–15
condemned to a life of discord.

Through the toil of laborers, unearned privileges are piled up, only nourishing strife and discord. Social distinctions and class consciousness rob people of soul and spirit. The injustice man commits daily against man arouses the wrath of the God of peace until it reaches white heat. The prophets of God expose the depravity of assessing human beings in terms of monetary value. We are all responsible for the condition of those who have hardly any human dignity or joy in life or vestige of peace left. As outcasts from the love of human society, they are delivered up to discord and unpeace.

The prophecy of peace takes a stand against whatever stifles or degrades love to humanity – that is, against the deadening of the social conscience. Prophecy rises up against the loveless will to possess. The prophet of peace attacks pride of rulership that makes slaves of others. The rich person's cold love of money and heartless will to possess – which result in economic exploitation of the poor – summon the prophets of peace to the battlefield of the spirit. The prophetic spirit breaks with all force and wealth. The prophet calls no one honest who gathers possessions at the expense of others and through violence.

The prophetic spirit calls to account all who helped trample the poor, who sided with the rich against those with nothing. The prophet Amos says every luxury is won at the expense of the poor and needy. The wealthy enjoy expensive furnishings, rich food and drink, and spacious rooms only through tyrannizing and crushing the poor and the needy. Other prophets, too, hurl their "Woe betide thee!" at those who, by amassing clothing and furniture from

James 5:1–6

Prov. 22:7–9

Matt. 19:23–24

Amos 2:6–8
Amos 4:1–3

Jer. 22:13–14

the poor through seizure, become enemies of their
own people: "You tear the skin from the body and the
flesh from the people's bones. You feed upon the flesh
of my people."

    The prophet exposes the enormous outrage of
people planning to gain new land and houses to
consolidate and increase private property. Isaiah
cries "Woe!" to all "who join house to house, lay field
to field until there is no place for others." Moses
had already spoken the word of the Lord: "The land
is mine." "The earth belongs to me." It must not
become heritable property. Taking interest, like
owning land, is unmasked as godlessness: they are
the two hands of greedy mammon. All taking of
interest is condemned by Ezekiel through God's
word: "You have forgotten me!"

    Ezekiel proclaims God's justice at work only where
no one is harassed by poor wages or demands for
money, where goods are not seized for debts, where
people give their bread to the hungry and their
clothes to the naked, where money is borrowed and
lent without interest: that is, where the right to own
property has been supplanted by love.

    All prophets want economic oppression overcome,
slavery's yoke removed, the degraded set free, the
homeless brought home, and the ill-clad given new
clothes. Hosea puts the prophetic demand into one
brief sentence: "Hold fast to love and justice and wait
steadfastly for God!" All prophets know that for this
to happen a new spirit has to come over humankind.
The Spirit of God must be poured out over the
crushed and downtrodden as well if their suffering
is to be removed. The God of the stars and all their

Mic. 3:1–3

Isa. 5:8

Lev. 25:23

Exod. 19:5

Ezek. 22:12

Ezek. 18:7–9

Isa. 58:3–7

Hos. 12:6

Isa. 42:1–7   heavenly hosts will rule on the earth. He has laid his
Spirit on the one whose righteousness and justice will
never be exhausted until firmly established over all
the earth as peace: it shall begin with one and shall
come upon all.

Swords will be beaten into tools

The Spirit-bearer will judge the lowly and wretched
justly and protect them, but he will overthrow the

Isa. 11:3–5   oppressors with the word of justice. He is called "The

Jer. 23:6   Lord is our righteousness." His justice and righteousness will bring peace; swords and spears will be
beaten into tools for peaceful work. No nation will lift
up weapons against another. No one will prepare for

Isa. 2:2–4   war anymore. The King of justice will obliterate all
war chariots and weapons, for the earth shall be filled

Isa. 11:9   with the knowledge of God as the waters fill the sea.

Through the centuries, the prophets' call for
justice resounds like an echo heralding the peace to
come. For thousands of years peace is the direction
of the prophets for the earth and humankind. This
call is more distinct than the stamping tread and
roar of all the wars of the world. The approaching
day of the Prince of Peace is mightier than any
throughout history. Human works come to a halt!
The work of God comes over humankind and over
the whole torn earth in final and all-embracing
peace! The work of God breaks straight in! It penetrates to the depths and spans the breadths! In the
midst of collapse, the Man of Peace arises without
whom no peace can be achieved.

The people of peace follow the Master of Peace,
whose nature is the lifeblood of their order of life.

His Spirit, who is for the lowly and against the great tyrants, inspires their unity. His Spirit of Peace opposes war. His journey of peace on the humblest beast of burden displaces cavalry, breaks the weapons of war, and inaugurates national peace. This Peace Bearer sets prisoners free and redeems the downtrodden. The majesty of his divine peace is framed by the princely forms of justice and well-being and by gracious kindness that shines out on the poor.

Zech. 9:9–10

Isa. 61:1–4

No peace and disarmament without social justice! No prophet recognizes peace and disarmament or the changing of deadly weapons into tools of civilization without social renewal and reconciliation that give back to the poor the use of all tools and products.

The prophet Moses had already proclaimed: "There shall be no poor among you!" Yet he knew there would be poor people in this world until every remnant of injustice had disappeared through the energies and hearts of all people being concentrated on peace, giving brotherly love unlimited authority. Because Jesus sees this approaching, he can and must say, "Blessed are the poor! Woe to the rich!"

Deut. 15:4

Luke 6:20–26

The majesty of God comes very near to this earth! Kindness and faithfulness, righteousness and well-being kiss each other. Faithfulness springs out of the earth! Righteousness comes down from heaven! Going out from people's hearts, peace penetrates into all lands because it comes down from God's highest heaven like lightning. It comes as justice. It reveals its clear and simple nature as the love expressed in fairness and brotherliness. This descending ball of lightning annihilates unpeace in its blazing flames.

Ps. 85:8–13

Isa. 64:1–4

Peace demands the abolition of wealth

When peace conquers, it means the abolition of wealth as much as of armed force. Both powers wield enormous influence, but faith stands against them and conquers. Faith meets with deeper understanding among the poor than among the rich. The will to peace is strongest and most genuine where poverty of goods goes hand in hand with the hunger and thirst of spiritual poverty. The kingdom of God will bring fairness and brotherliness and bind in complete unity all those whose longing hearts hunger for justice and righteousness. For this reason wealth and all surfeit of wealth must be dispersed.

Matt. 5:6

The prophets demand inflexibly that all ostentatious extravagance in clothing, housing, and social life be cut out, root and branch. Utmost simplicity shall be established in all things. Unity demands it. The style of unity is expressed in the beauty of the simple line. Social peace can be achieved in no other way. The circle and the straight line are symbols of the love that gathers and the genuine truth that goes with it. When no one outspends another, when no one embellishes life to suit his vanity, everyone will be drawn into the community of shining clarity. When privileges and luxury are abolished, justice has broken through.

Isa. 3:16–25

1 Tim. 6:6–12

By making rifts in society, social inequality destroys the sense of community and all possibility of community. It must be attacked with the sharpness of the Spirit if the cause of peace is to go forward. Luxury and greed, property and wealth are the roots of discord. So the beginning of the great prophecy of Amos mercilessly assails the unequal

distribution of the joys and goods of this world.
Hosea and all the other prophets follow his example
with the same sharpness.

Amos 5:10–13

What is true of the root is true of the fruit. The
violence of killing and warfare is and will always be
the height of unpeace, the bitterest fruit of injustice.
Isaiah therefore points to the law of peace: "The
violent shall be no more." But the peace of Christ's
justice shall never cease. The kingdoms of this world
shall all be destroyed because they are warlike kingdoms. Dominion, power, and might over all things
under heaven shall be given to the holy people of
the Most High, for they are the people of peace and
justice. The kingdoms of this world with their predatory nature will be swept away without distinction,
whether their emblem is the eagle, the lion, the bear,
or other beast of prey. The Son of Man has come to
destroy the works of the devil.

Isa. 29:20

Dan. 7:27

1 John 3:8

The hour of decision draws near: "Ask me, and I
will make the nations your inheritance, the ends of
the earth your possession." "May the nations be glad
and sing for joy, for you rule the peoples with equity
and guide the nations of the earth." "Say among the
nations: the Lord reigns. . . . He will judge the people
with equity. Let the heavens rejoice, let the earth
be glad." "The King is mighty, he loves justice." "He
crowns the humble with victory."

Ps. 2:8

Ps. 67:4

Ps. 96:10
Ps. 99:4
Ps. 149:4

Jesus fulfills the prophecies of peace
The new covenant takes up this proclamation and
makes it a reality, as Ezekiel had foretold: "I will make
them one nation in the land . . . and one king shall be
king over them all; and they shall be no longer two

Ezek. 37:22 nations, and no longer divided into two kingdoms."
In Christ, Isaiah's words became reality: "O you
afflicted one, tossed by the tempest, I will teach your
Isa. 54:11–13 children great peace. Violence shall no more be heard
Isa. 60:18 in your land, nor destruction within your borders."
In the church of Jesus Christ, Jeremiah's word is ful-
filled: "The days are coming when the city of the Lord
Jer. 31:38–40 shall be uprooted no more."

The Spirit of the new church says through Peter:
"Change from the root up! Make a complete turn in
your life! Your sins must be wiped out. Let the time
of new life break in! It comes from the presence of
the Lord of all worlds! The coming time sends the
Ruler! He will be announced to you beforehand. In
heavenly power, Jesus Christ waits until the time has
come when everything shall be fulfilled that God has
spoken by the mouth of all his holy prophets since the
Acts 3:19–21 world began."

Jesus Christ is the goal of human history. God's
prophecy with its all-commanding view proclaims
the final peace of Jesus Christ. In this peace all
enmity is extinguished, all war put down, and all
strife brought to an end. Christ is the beginning of
God-created humankind and its life-bringing end.
Isa. 41:4 He is the first and last of the living letters that spell
Rev. 21:5–6 out the divine plan of peace. In Jesus, the whole
course of history turns toward its conclusion, when
all things will be renewed. The long-awaited unity
of peace, approaching at last in Jesus, will lead in the
completely different, entirely new rule of God.

The kingdom of God draws near. God's will shall
at last prevail. The mystery of his name shall be
revealed by what is hidden in his heart. Jesus' first

and last concern, the entire content of his will to live
(which was also a readiness to die), was the glory
of God, that is, the glory of God's heart. Jesus, who
revealed the heart of God, knows that the future is
dedicated to it. From now on, all those who, in Christ,
believe in the future of God's heart are dedicated to
the absolute will of peace. Thus for the deeply longing
hearts of Jesus' inner circle, the first petitions of the
Lord's Prayer show the old covenant's prophecy of
peace endowed with new and final perfection: Thy   Matt. 6:9–10
name! Thy will! Thy kingdom!

Everything Jesus says and does makes real the
rule of peace foretold by the prophets and confirms
the truth of all their promises. In the church of Jesus   John 14:25–31
Christ, the long-prophesied community, bound by
common covenant, becomes reality now precisely
as it will in the coming kingdom. The word of the   Acts 4:32–35
prophets of old has paved the way for the messianic
rule of peace. Now from all nations, the future
citizens of the kingdom of peace stream together.
They gather around Christ. A call to the power and
holiness of perfect peace goes out from the church to   Matt. 28:18–20
the whole world.

God's people of old are and will be the starting
point for the new people of unity. Yet in Jesus all
national barriers have fallen and his kingdom of
unity spreads unimpeded. In the presence of the
uniting Spirit of the future, the divisive spirit of this
age is of no significance. Through the Spirit radiat-
ing from the church, all national boundaries are
abolished forever. The heirs of the old covenant, now   Eph. 2:11–20
consecrated in Christ, extend the work of peace over
the whole earth. All land belongs to God. Jesus has   Acts 3:25

burned his fiery rule of peace from the other world into this world.

In Jesus Christ, the fiery spirit of the old prophecy of peace comes to perfect expression for all time. It starts in the present: the peace foretold by the prophets penetrates into the church of Christ as love, justice, and truth, present here and now down to their last consequences. Jesus, like all the prophets, knows no reconciliation with destructive opposition. His prophetic truth knows no giving in or making of concessions. He does not work for peace by making compromises. His peace makes no covenant with

2 Cor. 6:14–16 unpeace. He never joins any hostile opposition. He destroys unpeace. His opposition to the roots of unpeace is inexorable.

The Sermon on the Mount shows the way

Jesus, sparing none, hurls his sevenfold woe at the

Matt. 23:13–39 hypocritical destroyers of all true unity. Their answer is murderous. As foretold by the prophets, every government and all powers of world economics are bound to fight with the most deadly violence against the perfect expression of peace in Jesus Christ and his church. In this way, the character of unconditional peace shines out more strongly and clearly than ever and delivers up the peace bearers, unarmed, to the flaming sword of the enemy. Jesus' Sermon on the Mount, the most powerful prophecy of the kingdom of peace, stands for the will to peace with its resistance unto death – any death. Against the peace-disrupting power of the whole world it sets the passive resistance of the cross: the cross versus the sword!

The cross is the radicalism of love. The peace of the Sermon on the Mount tackles everything at the root. Out of love it gives away the last remnants of property, down to jacket and shirt, and gives every bit of working strength to the community spirit of absolute unity. As often as love demands it, this peace sacrifices itself and goes serenely twice the distance and gives twice the working time required. Without pause, the church of peace conducts an active and creative general strike against all the surrounding injustice of outward unpeace. In this break with the status quo, Jesus recognizes no claims justified by law. He does not allow his church to carry on any lawsuit or to sit in judgment in any court of law. He demands that the church should drop or interrupt its religious worship whenever brothers need to be reconciled, whenever the genuineness of brotherly unity is in question. He places the restoring and maintaining of the unity of love over and against the insincere cult of disunited piety.

Matt. 5:40-48

Matt. 7:1-5

Matt. 5:23-25

In his Sermon on the Mount, Jesus gives an absolute mandate never to resist the power of evil. Only thus can evil be turned to good. Jesus' will to love would rather be struck twice than counter with even one blow. Love matters more than anything else. Love allows no other feelings to come in. In marriage, too, love keeps faith and fights against any separation or divorce. Because it is forgiveness, love governs private prayer. As complete reconciliation, this absolute and all-embracing will to love determines our attitude to society (to our enemy as well – yes, particularly to him). Love does not take the slightest part in hostilities, strife, or war, nor can it ever

Matt. 5: 38-39

Matt. 5:27-32
Matt. 6:6

return curses and hate, hurt and enmity – neither
in the individual nor in the community. Love is
not influenced by any hostile power. No change of
circumstance can change the attitude of Jesus and his
followers; he does nothing but love, make peace, wish
and ask for good, and work good deeds. Where the
peace of Jesus Christ dwells, war dies out, weapons
are melted down, and hostility vanishes. Love has
become boundless in Jesus; it has achieved absolute
sovereignty.

Here at last the justice and righteousness begun
in the prophets becomes complete reality. The
righteousness of Jesus Christ is better than that of
all moralists and theologians and of all socialists,
communists, and pacifists, for in it flows the life-sap
of the living planting of a future of perfect peace.
Here the salt of the divine inner nature is at work in
strength. Here the light of God's heart streams out as
the beacon of the city-church whose towers proclaim
freedom, unity, and dedication. Here what people
want for themselves, they want for everyone. Here no
one lays up private possessions, and people's hearts
are not cold with icy fear for their own existence or
how to make ends meet. Here the peace of love reigns.

Matt. 5:13–17
Matt. 7:12

Matt. 6:19–34

Unity will provoke opposition

In this city-church, all citizens gather with one goal
in mind: God's will and God's rule, God's heart and
God's nature. No one is in opposition to another here
and no one is condemned. Here no one is coerced,
no one is despised, and no one is violated. And
yet love rules as truth, and the nature of people's
inmost hearts is recognized by the fruits, by deeds.

Matt. 7:16–27

Here everybody knows well that such a determined common will provokes the sharpest opposition from the surrounding world. Perfect unity, which gathers and binds, is seen as a provocation. People view it as enmity toward humankind and the nation, an infuriating exclusiveness. It makes all those resentful who, like most people, feel that they are neither able nor willing to accept the call to such complete community. So a clash is inevitable. No one can escape it.

This living community of hearts, this combining of goods and working strength, stands out in absolute contrast to the attitude of the whole world. This is bound to cause resentment, especially in those whose ideals drive them to violent action for which they want support. For in this community of love every hostile act is rejected, whatever the circumstances and however weighty the reasons. Any participation in warlike action, police activity, or law proceedings is out of the question, however justified it may seem on the grounds of protecting the good. This community of peace has nothing in common with violent revolt, however necessary it may seem in the name of suppressed justice. The very fact that such a life exists, symbolizing the kingdom of peace and love, challenges all (both right and left) who regard government by force as the primary duty of the hour.

Because the expectation of the coming peaceable kingdom leads people to a life in full community, all those who look upon community as impossible are affronted by it. As long as they are determined to refuse the continuing fellowship of the wedding feast, Matt. 22:2–14 as long as they cannot accept what is so great and yet so intimate – the bond of peace, the common table, the unity of life, the cooperation in work, and the church that carries responsibility – they have no other choice than to fight it. In the end, though reluctantly, they take measures to destroy it. So, in spite of the church's unconditional stand for peace in all situations, severe struggles and clashes are bound to result from the will to community, precisely because of its uncompromising nature. These clashes are bound to grow in number and intensity the nearer the church of peace draws to the final kingdom of peace.

In the church, the beginning of the coming kingdom is present in full force with challenging clarity. Before the final spread of the rule of peace, there has to be a last battle between the power of strife and discord and the strongest power, the power of peace. The severity and dreadfulness of the last battles will be more and more startling as the peace witness of the church reaches its consummation and her martyrs once more go unarmed to their death. But under no circumstances can the opposition be left in repose. For there, people will not give up their selfish separation as individuals or as national groups. People cannot or will not let the root of sin, of curse-laden unpeace, be taken away from them. They maintain that it is absolutely indispensable.

People cannot trust peace. They want nothing of faith, and reject the better future. They would rather trust the idols of brute force than the spirit of love and the God of peace. Property needs the protection of law and force. People want to hold on to what belongs to them, and will not accept anything from others. They demand their rights and reject grace. Under the law, sin continues and unpeace remains.

John 15:17–21
Matt. 10:17–22

Matt. 24:6–14

Jer. 17:5–8

Rom. 13:1–4

Rom. 7:7–9

The law's iron hand holds on to bloody judgment
and the sword, striking individuals and mowing
down whole nations with its ghastly weapons, which
poison continents and will in the end destroy the
whole earth. Sin and the law make death inevitable.
Finally God himself, against the ultimate will of his
heart, must assent to this judgment of wrath, which is
necessary according to the justice of the law.

James 1:15

War is a deserved judgment

When the peoples harden their hearts against the
one and only way willed by God in his pure love, they
call down judgment on themselves as a matter of
natural necessity. Then the most unnatural outcomes
result inevitably, as a kind of unavoidable natural
disaster, from their own actions. This happens when
people despise God's creative will in sexuality, with
the result that he must give them over to impure
and degrading degeneracy in their sexual lives. This
happens, too, when people willingly reject the will to
peace, with the result that the fierce flames of war,
brother against brother, must rage over them. God
in his wrath brings on the judgment precipitated by
self-will. The old state of affairs is repeated: God in
his wrath once gave his beloved people a warlike king
because, in their war-lust and greed for the status of a
major power, they had rejected his own kingship. Still
earlier, God's law had allowed blood vengeance and
the death penalty to replace the rejected leadership
of the Spirit, and the Flood had buried the flesh that
had turned away from the spirit. Thus will God's
judgment let the fiery flood of war break in over this
Christ-hating unpeace, which now craves its own
ultimate escalation.

Eph. 5:5–6

Rom. 1:24–27

Hos. 13:10–11

Lev. 24:19–22
Gen. 6:13

2 Pet. 3:7–10

This fate is inescapable: it is a matter of cause and effect. War is the karma, the necessary consequence, of discord, unpeace, and lack of community. It is the deadly fruit of the broken fellowship with God. It is the inescapable judgment over the causes of war: separation from God's unity, division of life into hostile opposites, and injustice and disunity arising from property and selfishness. War judges itself. It is based on unpeace with God and disunity among people. War is the monstrosity born of the covetous will, the hell of disunity. War intensifies this compulsion to sin to the point of self-destruction. It drives the law, which kills, to the point of massacring nations. In war, loveless injustice surpasses itself. It becomes murderous lawlessness.

James 4:1–3

War is the insane culmination of the clash between judging law and unbridled lawlessness; its ultimate purpose is to reveal sin. The judgment of war must crash down on humankind, hammering and shaping us so that at last a longing arises for the cause of death to be overcome, for community in God to become everything. To be rid of war, the roots of sin must be exposed and eradicated. Once the cause of separation is overcome, unity and community will break in. Then not a hand will be lifted, not a foot will be stirred, to serve the monstrosity of hell that is called war. With sin destroyed, brothers are no longer killed. The way ahead is made free, and in the empty space, the peace of God arises. Repentance gives birth to faith; faith brings peace. Ending separation to establish unity – that is the gospel.

Rom. 5:1, 12–21

1 Cor. 15:56

To sin belongs the law. To law belongs killing. These three uphold each other. Jesus Christ, through the Holy Spirit and in the name of God, has

conquered this triple alliance of death for ever and
ever. He broke the weapon of death – sin. He tore
up the writ of accusation and judgment. His death
unmasked the origin of all killing: he tore out its root
cause. He plants resurrection and the unity of the
Holy Spirit in the places where dissolution, separation, and sin are eradicated.

Rom. 8:1–2, 21

Col. 2:13–15

The Law of Moses brought war, which it then had
to control. The grace and truth of the gospel bring
unity and the order of community. Because national
and international laws determine the prosecution of
illegal conduct, they require war, imprisonment, and
death. The sons of Christ's Spirit keep peace, bring
freedom, and grant forgiveness of sins. Through the
mission of the Spirit, they spread abroad unity of life.

John 1:17

James 1:25

Where Christ takes over the government, the rule
of all other death-dealing powers is annulled. Where
the Spirit rules with grace, the law of governmental
authority withdraws. Death's judgment retreats
before the salvation and resurrection of life. Gathering replaces enmity. So it is in the church, and so
it will be at the end when the first and last fruit of
separation from God, death itself, is swept away. All
the works of enmity will be destroyed and, last of
all, the final enemy himself. Before then, all enmity
and hostility must be given up; it leads to death. The
auxiliary troops of death will be the first to be surrounded; first the tree with its roots will be torn up.
Then the poisonous fruits of death will be attacked to
the very last seed, till death itself is done away with.

1 Cor. 15:24–26

Rev. 20:14

However, evil and murder are still on the increase,
gaining more and more influence. The stronger the
power of love grows, the more it drives poisonous
hostility to a peak. The reverse is also true. When

evil has matured, it is time to clear out what has
ripened in death's plantation and make room for the
Matt. 13:30 laying-out of God's garden. This dual development
of completely opposed events forces decision. It leads
to a tearing down and to a new building up. The
course of all history runs up from below and down
from above. From both directions it converges on a
single point. Apostolic prophecy [in the Revelation]
follows this dual line of development to the end.
The point where they meet is the end: the judgment and the kingdom. Both lines are drawn by
"religiously" motivated hands: "satanism" and "faith"
are the mysterious forces that direct this dual line of
development.

Both church and state oppose peace

Siding with the deadly power of evil, the godlessness
of a life of hypocrisy and murderous corruption
mounts to the maddest heights of arrogance: with
amazing pomp and splendor, it claims the highest
place of all in the house of God. It is the false prophecy of the church that has fallen away from God,
which hypocritically flaunts the raiment and the mien
of the animal of peace, like a sacrificial lamb, while
making propaganda for the dragon of war. In the form
Rev. 13:11–18 of a lamb it speaks like the dragon and stands against
the Lamb. To wage war against the church of peace,
it joins forces with the warring monster of worldly
power, the power of all armed nations.

The church of peace sets out against this overwhelming and twofold power without the protection
of murderous weapons. She refuses to worship either
power and knows that the high and mighty Babylon

will fall. Certainly, this false and faithless woman   Rev. 14:8
is still firmly seated on the throne of the world's
ruling powers and authorities. Elated by power, she
is still intoxicated with the blood of the martyrs she
has sacrificed. But the breath of the coming reign of   Rev. 17:6
Christ sweeps her off. The twofold world power from
below is broken from above. The lying dragon of
unpeace is expelled and war is banned. The reign of   Rev. 17–20
peace comes.

The last outburst of war from humankind's major
powers storms out of the night. Like every war, it
bears afresh the marks of Satan's power let loose and
so is bound to assault the kingdom of God once more
before it is overthrown. This final war, this last world
conflagration, must annihilate forever all states based
on force and all major world powers. The new eon
begins by putting a final end to all the powers of war.
The joyous unity of the wedding banquet and the
table fellowship of the love feast replace the horrors of
war, enmity, and death.

In solitary greatness amidst a world full of
enemies, the prophets of old were impelled to
increase their opposition to the priesthood of the
established religion of their day and to the sovereigns
of their state – all this to the same degree that these   Dan. 6:13
two powers expanded their double-faced rule along
the lines of the great heathen powers with all their
wars and magnificent pomp. In the same way, the
apostolic prophets of early Christianity have had to
fight with ever-increasing ardor against the bloody
violence of political power and against all religion
that hypocritically supports them but in truth has   Mark 12:38–40
fallen away from God.

Even in judgment, God's aim is peace

To the prophets, the God of Abraham is and always will be the God of the kingdom. According to the faith of the apostles, the Father of Jesus Christ does not want to be forever a God of the law. He is the same God as he was at the time of the lawgiver and prophet Moses, but the way of his heart triumphs over the ways of his wrath. The Spirit of his peace supersedes the law. What the law could not achieve, God accomplished in Christ. Through Christ's Spirit, faith in the God and Father of Jesus Christ is obedient to peace, because faith when it is perfected has as its object the God of perfect love. It is the God of history who makes all the threads of history run together and come to an end in the one, single way of peace – the peace of his Christ.

We must distinguish between the innermost heart of God and his waist that is girded with judgment. For hidden in the somber flames of judgment lives the ray of his pure love. The deadly accurate judgment of his presence is nearer to love than the cold distance of a god who hides his face. The brazen footsteps of God's wrath are dreadful. It is a terrible thing to fall into the hands of his judgment. But secretly his pulsing heart spreads out a mantle of love for all his enemies. Beautiful are the feet of his messengers, spreading joy as they come from the mountains and bring the message of God's heart to the valley of judgment. Their greeting to everyone is peace. Their message is clear: the judgment of God is fulfilled in his heart. He himself has been met by it. God's heart becomes king! His ambassadors wept bitterly because peace had been lost. For them, there is no harsher judgment than the loss of peace. But now

Ps. 105:7–11

Rom 10:4

James 2:22

Isa.11:5

Heb. 10:30–31

Isa. 52:7

Isa. 33:7

they hand over this sealed message: that miracle, the
heart, is stronger than all judgment. 1 John 3:19–20

Though mountains melt in volcanic eruptions and
hills be laid low by appalling earthquakes – even if the
earth itself should totter and crack and the judgment
of his mighty wrath demolish great powers – still, the
love of God's heart, the rainbow of his perfection,
will never waver. The sun of his heart shines upon
the devastating storm-curtain of his wrath and the
rainbow of peace spans it. Even if leagues of nations Ps. 46
and world peace itself suffer shipwreck and all treaties be torn up, the seal of God's covenant will not
break. Times of judgment will come and sink into
the grave. But peace will arise and remain. That will
not change. Peace is God's final word; it is his heart.
Peace is and always will be the ultimate will of God.

If we stop looking merely at the historical instruments of judgment, at the human vessels of wrath,
and with deep discernment turn to the heart of God,
which is at the heart of his works throughout history,
then in spite of the murderous chaos of war and the
injustice raging around us, we have entered into the
garden of peace. The historical Jesus is the heart of
God. As the coming Christ, he shows the importance John 3:16
of God's heart for the whole world. His command
empowers us to sheath the sword and put it away
forever. The heart of Jesus foresees with fearful Matt. 26:52
clarity the catastrophe ahead that will devastate
all the kingdoms of this earth and the whole world
economy through major international wars and
bloody revolutions. He knows that because of strife
and discord, the hour of wrath must precede the Day
of Peace. The approaching fall of civilization with the
final war of judgment is one of the main themes of

Matt. 24
Rev. 13
2 Thess. 2
Matt. 13:24–30
2 Tim. 3:1–5
Rev. 13:10
Rev. 20:4

his great prophetic speech, which John and Paul have enlarged upon so powerfully in apostolic prophecy.

The dreadful cup cannot be avoided. The plowland must be cleared; the corrupting weeds must be burned. After they have run riot for the last time, they must never again be able to spread their seeds of murder. If evil is to be uprooted, it must be exposed for what it is. Political chaos, outbursts of war and revolution, economic depressions, and frightful natural catastrophes shall once more deliver humankind to the knife of its own unpeace. But in the midst of all the hellish tumult, the paradise of peace is revealed. Those who hold out and shed no blood in spite of the mounting horrors of the final desolation, doing God's holy work in pure, brotherly love, will come through the sharpest judgment and the last catastrophe.

The old world collapses in terrible self-destruction, but the church of Jesus Christ takes no part in all this horror. The frenzied power of the world loathes the unassailable peace stand of Christ's church. In their fury, all warlike powers persecute the gathered unity of God's peace. Even in the battering storm of extreme need, the church rejects the slightest sign of the militarism of the inhuman beast of prey. The power of love opposes the violence of unpeace. Precisely for this reason, persecution reaches the heights of its fury. The prophetic Spirit of the King of Peace sees that the tension between these ultimate and diametrically opposed powers of love and hate is the shaking force at work everywhere in world history and in history's end. This Spirit sees that the throes of extreme need must precede the birth of world peace.

The dreadful birth pangs of the end times are part of the curse of death brought by the loss of man's

original peace. The peace of God and of the great
Advent cannot be born without a final judgment over
frightening unpeace as it brings forth its last monstrosity. Just before the new breaks in, all that is old
must be shattered by appalling need. All institutions
made by human society must be overthrown. Every
form of their power and slavery must be obliterated.
No peace can be planted on the unchanged soil of
unpeace. The plow sets to work. It breaks up the
sod again. The beginning of God's rule leads to the
frightening end of world history so that on its ruins,
purified of all adulteration, the justice and righteousness of eternal peace will be able to rise.

Rom. 8:18–23

The kingdom breaks in now

Right into the midst of a world driven frantic with
unpeace and injustice, Christ will let the unblemished
kingdom of peace break in. But this future, coming
directly from above, is already present in the Spirit
of Jesus Christ: in his church, the will to peace is put
into practice here and now. God's world judgment,
advancing through the last and greatest catastrophe
in the history of war, annihilates the evil powers of
discord in order to bring in eternal peace. God's rule
has to make this final step because it cannot make
any alliance with the powers of injustice. Under the
trampling boots of soldiers, God's heart, as Christ
crucified once again, beats on in unchanging love:
it is the church of the Crucified One, which carries
God's peace inviolate to meet the coming Day.

1 Pet. 2:20–21

Col. 1:24

The Spirit of Jesus Christ lets the fresh air of the
ultimate kingdom of peace blow into the midst of
this sultry, disaster-laden atmosphere. His gospel
brings purity, reconciliation, and unity. His new

Spirit is the authentication of the kingdom of peace.
Through the signet and seal of the Spirit, what is
decreed for the future is already entrusted to the
church. The church of Jesus Christ is the body of the
community of perfect peace, through which life and
immortality are revealed in our time. As the bearer
of the kingdom of peace, the church is freed from all
killing and murdering.

When we are gathered in the church and God's
love fills our hearts, we cannot be tempted by any
power that belongs to force. As Jesus can never be
thought of as a Roman soldier, so members of his
church can never be chiefs of police, air force officers,
artillerymen, or policemen. Neither poison nor bombs
nor pistols nor knives, neither the executioner's sword
nor the gallows can be our weapons. As the revelation
of the heart of Jesus, as Christ's letter, our task is
simply to pass on the image of absolute love in all its
clarity. Standing in the presence of Christ, we must
represent that he has arrived; when Christ reveals
himself now, we must proclaim his future coming.

What is invisible in the world of peace to come
becomes visible in the church. Everyone shall see
this work of God. Everyone shall honor the Father
of Jesus Christ through it. This unadulterated image
of Jesus is the only hope for the future. The church
is his uplifted torch, the radiant city on the hill. The
stars of prophecy have shone through the night of
unpeace. For centuries they have moved across the
celestial sphere of world history. As history draws to a
close, the starry heavens of prophecy will let the great
gods of military power spread their twilight. When
the days were fulfilled, the morning star of the King

Rom. 8:6, 17

2 Tim. 1:10

Rom. 8:35–39

2 Cor. 3:2–3

1 Cor. 11:26

John 17

of Peace rose in the firmament of prophecy. As the
morning star of the church, he heralds the dawn of
the coming day. The church is wedded to the sun of
peace. Those who let the morning star rise in their
hearts are freed from all warlike powers of this world
and belong with every beat of their hearts to the
coming day of God's great peace.

2 Pet. 1:16–19

The dawn of the new age lights up the invisible
city of peace. The hidden land of community appears.
In the Holy Spirit of the church, the New Jerusalem
comes down from above. Only the perfect city
without a temple has done away with cultic religion.
In this city, community life is the temple of peace, the
temple of the great King. The church bears the seven
lamps of the Sabbath of peace, on which man's own
works shall rest forever because the mighty, silent
works of God have begun. The city of peace and joy
reveals the radiant brightness of the new creation.
The old order has passed away. The new order comes
into force. Everything becomes new.

Rev. 21

Exod. 25:31–40

Rev. 1:12–13

Heb. 4:3–11

This is the gathering from the four winds, from the
ends of the earth to the ends of heaven, the uniting
of those still alive with those living in glory – God's
kingdom of peace. Its power in the future begins in
the unchangeable community of life and spirit, which
in our time bears the name "church." In the peace of
the city-church, the bride prepares herself to receive
her bridegroom. She will go to his wedding feast carrying the blazing torches of the Spirit.

Mark 13:27

This feast day of the King of Peace establishes the
throne of his government; his infinite joy makes it
possible for his reign to begin. The places of work for
his kingdom are already there; will and deed crown

his feast. When people celebrate their freedom from the hideous monster of bloody violence and from the powerful woman of seduction and unfaithfulness, a fruitful life arises with a clear authority. On the foundation of the Atonement, which brings unity and enthusiasm, the reign of the priestly king begins, inaugurated by his feast. It is a feast celebrating the perfected reign of peace, for which the bride of the king has prepared herself.

Rev. 13:11–17
Rev. 17:1–6
Rev. 21:1–3

This message of apostolic prophecy was entrusted to John as certain tidings of the approaching time. It is "the revelation given to Jesus Christ by God to show his servants what must very soon take place." The Christ who appears among the seven lampstands of the church receives the book of the future from the sovereign of the world, who is surrounded by the twenty-four elders and the four radiant living creatures of the star-world. Only he who is the faith of the church is able to open the book. Thus his present is the ultimate future of the dawning kingdom of peace. This is true in the church, so that John had to write his revelation to the seven churches as a reality in the present and a certainty for the future: what exists now is a picture of what shall be hereafter. To the seer whose eyes are open, faith's present and hope's future are one and the same. What unites them is love.

Rev. 1:1
Rev. 4:4–8
Rev. 1:19–20

In the church of the Holy Spirit, the future kingdom of God is present with its perfect justice, its absolute peace, and its joy in love and unity. In the midst of the church, the King of Peace brings here and brings now her inviolable community of peace both within and without – nothing but peace. Where there is redemption and reconciliation through

Rom. 14:17–19

Christ, even the locking-up of Satan for the thousand years of rejoicing is present reality because peace is now and here put into action. The church is the door of peace, open in the present as an entrance into the kingdom of the future. So for the believing and united church, Satan is already bound; in the church, his divisiveness and hostility have been done away with. The kingdom of peace has been won. Weapons are laid down. Christ is king now and he is king here as the head and the heart of the church.

Rev. 20

Matt. 12:28

Rev. 17:14

The church sends out bearers of light

From the church, Christ's spirit of love and his will to unity press outward into all the world. This present fact guarantees certainty about the future: he is the one to conquer and renew all creation, to make the whole torn cosmos into a new and living unit. In Christ the old world passes, and the new creation arises. Jesus is the new man of the church, as the Son of Man in the coming kingdom. In Jesus, God's rule has now, through faith, become love to our brothers and to our enemies. For those who have eyes of faith to see, the life in his church shall be the living parable of the unity and peace for which God wants to conquer the earth. In the church, the world of today can see the image of the city of peace. It is the signpost to the future, and everyone will see it. No corner on earth is to be left in darkness; the light, held aloft, floods into all rooms. The city of light sends out bearers of light. Community in the city on the hill and constant traveling for the sake of mission are identical.

Col. 1:19–20

2 Cor. 5:17

Matt. 5:14–16

The unity of the early Christian church and the apostleship of peace are one. From churches formed

in brotherly love, power is sent out to all inhabitants
of the earth – the power to create peace and harmony.
Rays from the small sun-city light up the whole
world. From apostolic times, the early Christian
church has been assigned the world-embracing task
to see that the one cause of the kingdom of God
should shine out in all directions with unalloyed
clarity. She is to represent nothing else. Not only did
the generation immediately following the apostles
make this abundantly clear: through succeeding gen-
erations the clear light of the original Christian truth
checked the slow but persistent growth of darkness
until well into the third century.

Matt. 10:5–40

The early Christians stood for peace
The post-apostolic elders of the earliest times took
the apostolic mission as their authority. About the
year AD 150, Justin held that the future proclaimed
by the prophets had already begun with the apostles.
That swords should be beaten into plowshares and
lances into sickles, that nation should no longer lift up
sword against nation, and that people should forget
how to wage war – for him all that had already begun.
As he writes, "From Jerusalem" – from the city-church
of absolute unity and perfect brotherliness – "there
went out into the world men, twelve in number, and
these illiterate, of no ability in speaking: but by the
power of God they proclaimed to every race of men
that they were sent by Christ to teach to all the word
of God." They came to convey the word of God to all
people as the reality of the perfect peace, in which we
"refrain from making war upon our enemies."[2]

Isa. 2:4

1 Cor. 2:4–5

---

2 Justin Martyr, ca. 100–ca.165, *First Apology* 39.

Justin describes early Christian life around AD 160 in just the same way, as an expression of reverence, justice, love to all people, and confident expectation of the future. Here again he testifies: "We who were filled with war and mutual slaughter and every wickedness have each through the whole earth changed our warlike weapons – our swords into ploughshares and our spears into implements of tillage."[3]

Theophilus writes still more strongly to Autolycus around AD 180: "We are forbidden so much as to witness shows of gladiators, lest we become partakers and abettors of murders. But neither may we see the other spectacles, lest our eyes and ears be defiled, participating in the utterances there sung." Not only every outward but also every inner participation in war is impossible. Any kind of propaganda for the glory of shedding blood is rejected. For in the church of Jesus Christ, "righteousness is exercised, law administered, worship performed, God acknowledged: truth governs, grace guards, peace screens them; the holy word guides, wisdom teaches, life directs, God reigns."[4]

At the end of this early period, Origen writes in no uncertain terms about what the consequences of this attitude of faith were for the early Christians: "Jesus nowhere teaches that it is right for his own disciples to offer violence to any one, however wicked. For he did not deem it in keeping with such laws as his, which were derived from a divine source, to allow the killing of any individual whatever."[5] His church has a

3 Justin, *Dialogue with Trypho* 110.

4 Theophilus of Antioch, died ca. 183, *To Autolycus* III.15.

5 Origen of Alexandria, ca. 184–ca. 253, *Against Celsus* III.7.

completely different public responsibility from that of the military and judicial power of state authority, a completely different political task, a completely different citizenship, and a completely different form of community life.

2 Cor. 10:3–4

For this reason, according to Tertullian (whose influence, like Origen's, continued into the third century) the holder of a government office could be regarded as a Christian only if he exercised his duty "neither sitting in judgment on anyone's life or character . . . ; neither condemning nor fore-condemning; binding no one, imprisoning or torturing no one."[6] In spite of the ascendance of the institutional church, the third century still held the same view as Athenagoras in the second century, who expressed it in these sharp words: "This is to feed upon human flesh, to do violence (in contravention of the very laws which you and your ancestors, with due care for all that is fair and right, have enacted) . . . against those to whom it even is not lawful, when they are struck, not to offer themselves for more blows, nor when defamed not to bless."[7]

As late as the year AD 248, Origen wrote that military service should not be demanded of Christians.[8] This attitude was still as clear to post-apostolic Christians as it had been to the early Christians of the first church. Since the emperor did not demand military service of priests, Origen argued, neither would the Christians go to the battlefield, not even when the emperor demanded it. Christians would

---

6 Tertullian, ca. 155–ca. 240, *On Idolatry* 17.

7 Athenagoras of Athens, ca. 130–ca. 190, *A Plea for the Christians* 34.

8 Origen, *Against Celsus* VIII.73.

support the governmental authorities only through
their prayer, which is determined by Christ; only
through prayer for peace; only through prayer for the
community of the new humanity; only in the prayer
that all inhabitants of the earth shall be given peace
and harmony; only in the request that the govern-
ments of all nations shall exercise their authority with
reverence, in peace and benevolence and without
violence; and only in the faith that the peace of a new   1 Tim. 2:1–2
life is brought about by the power of the resurrection
from the dead.

The First Letter of Clement (written before AD
100 yet strictly in line with the institutional church)
and also the much less ecclesiastical Acts of Thomas,
written soon after AD 160, express complete agreement with Origen. Justin, too, declared that all the
kingdoms and powers of the world look upon Jesus
with fear and yet must recognize that everywhere
believers in Christ are peace bringers. Moreover,
around AD 150 Justin wrote, "More than all other
men are we your helpers and allies in promoting
peace."[9] Tertullian sums up the attitude of early
Christianity from the time of the apostles right
into the third century with the words: "There is no
agreement between the divine and the human sacra-
ment, the standard of Christ and the standard of the
devil. . . . How will a Christian war, nay, how will he
serve even in peace, without a sword, which the Lord
has taken away?"[10]

---

9 Justin, *First Apology* 12.

10 Tertullian, *On Idolatry* 19.

Abortion and amassing wealth are also war

War is in fact the most powerful act of violence,
arising from a demonic power everywhere at work.
Under the banner of war, measures of the most
murderous kind (coming from a hostility that even
without war is constantly present) are carried so
far that they become an unbridled storm. "World
peace" is a state of war waged by other means;
it is not peace. Not only war is satanic; so is the
root of war – unpeace in times of political "peace."
Under the false name of peace, it commits demonic
crimes against life in every area. The outbreak of
military hostilities in civil and international war
is not by any means the only evil which the peace
bearers of the church must take a stand against.
They must stand as much against the widespread
damage done in private life, seen most clearly in
the destruction of nascent life, which was labeled
"murder" and "child-murder" by early Christian
writers. They called murderers those who "use
drugs to bring on abortion"[11] or who in tacit agreement allow it to be done to them.

Mic. 3:4–8

Bearers of peace are familiar with all the murky
sources of death-bringing division. They fight
money's power to buy and rule as passionately as they
fight unfaithfulness in love relationships because they
see there the dangerous seat of murderous unpeace.
Tertullian testifies that "all things are common
among us but our wives."[12] In essence, the dragon's
teeth of covetousness, in privileged ownership and
in unfaithful love relationships, is the power at
the root of the widespread state of war – latent or

---

11 Athenagoras, *A Plea for the Christians* 35.

12 Tertullian, *Apology* 39.

active – between people who are all meant to live a pure life together in God as brothers and sisters.

Money, according to the prophetic faith of early Christianity, is a "source of impiety, confusion's guide, a means of wars, an enemy of peace. / . . . / Those wishing it possess the nursing earth. / They waste the poor, that they themselves more land / procuring may enslave them by deceit."[13] Then justice can never be achieved, and peace is a sheer impossibility. Without justice or love, peace cannot last a moment.

According to this early Christian prophecy (which gained widespread recognition) and according to Justin's testimony, what is important is the power that proclaims the approaching time for people to live a brotherly life together on the land God has promised them. Defying death, the martyrs declared before their prosecutors that they could recognize no kingdom of this present world age and that they knew only one Lord, the king of all kings and ruler over all nations. In the third century still, according to Hippolytus, the conditions of acceptance into the early Christian church decreed that anyone should be rejected or excluded who was unwilling to refuse all killing, even killing required by law.[14] From all this it is clear how state power and the church were bound to provoke in each other the sharpest opposition.

Hermas, an exceptionally sober-minded prophet influential in Rome in post-apostolic times (perhaps before AD 100 but certainly before AD 155), summarizes this state of affairs in the following urgent challenge:

---

13 *Sibylline Oracles* VIII, 29–39.

14 *Apostolic Tradition* 16, an early church order attributed to Hippolytus of Rome, ca. 170–ca. 235.

You know that you who are servants of God are living in a foreign country, for your city is far from this city. If, therefore, you know your city in which you are destined to live, why do you prepare fields and expensive possessions and buildings and useless rooms here? If you are preparing these things for this city, you obviously are not planning to return to your own city. Foolish and double-minded and miserable person, do you not realize that all these things are foreign to you, and under someone else's authority? . . . So what are you going to do, since you are subject to the law of your own city? For the sake of your fields and the rest of your possessions, will you totally renounce your own law and live according to the law of this city? Take care; it may not be in your best interest to renounce your law, for if you should want to return to your city, you will certainly not be accepted, because you have renounced the law of your city, and will be shut out of it. So take care; as one living in a foreign land, do not prepare for yourself one thing more than is necessary to be self-sufficient, and be prepared so that whenever the master of this city wants to expel you because of your opposition to his law, you can leave his city and come to your own city, and joyfully conform to your law, free from all insult.[15]

Inner peace creates outward peace
Such stringent demands can only be made where people's hearts are alive with the spirit of perfect love and completely filled with the highest calling, that of the kingdom of God. The peace stand taken by

Rom. 12:11–21

---

15 *The Shepherd of Hermas* 50, from *The Apostolic Fathers*, trans. by Michael W. Holmes (Grand Rapids, MI: Baker Academic, 2007), 557–559.

the early Christians is possible only in the strength of the Gospels. Only where the call to the church of peace takes over the whole of life can concentration on mission lead to a break with the status quo. Only where the Spirit of Unity establishes inmost peace can the fight be ventured upon for peace and against unpeace all over the world.

Only in the church of Jesus Christ is that center of life-energy given which makes this stand possible. Peace with God makes the will to peace among people a reality. Without this will and without the working of Christ's peace, it is impossible to stand up against all the powers of the world. Only peace of heart in the unity of the church sets people free from obviously prevailing unpeace. Where inner peace is granted, it creates outer peace.

The harmony of united hearts calls forth, through the working together of all powers, peace's maximum achievements, possible only in the church. "Without peace of heart, nothing great will be achieved."[16] Only when the heart finds peace in the center of this gathering and uniting can it gain the impetus to go out far and wide from this one united whole. Without peace of heart, all our efforts are bound to work against each other; every good influence will be counteracted by its opposite. For this reason, no one should approach the question of nonviolence until he is truly decided to take up God's peace as the peace of the church, found in the gospel of Jesus Christ and given in the power of the Holy Spirit.

Peace means the greatest power possible, a gathering centered in God. Pestalozzi has described this

Eph. 4:1–16

John 16:33

---

16 Friedrich Heinrich Jacobi, 1743–1819, "Fliegende Blätter," *Minerva: Taschenbuch für das Jahr 1817.*

basic requisite for all education with these words: "Faith in God is the source of peace in life, peace in life is the source of inner order, inner order is the source of an undistracted use of our powers, order in the employment of our powers becomes in turn the source of the growth and development of our powers toward wisdom."[17] Peace of heart leads to unity in the church, whose spiritual order brings all powers into action in the right way and at the right time.

Rom. 12:4–8

Our powers grow in the harmony of working together. Peace has a divine wisdom that gives shape to a fruitful life, ordered in brotherly community. As long as we are still separate, we cannot experience

Eph. 2:13–19

this harmony. Separation from God is the cause of unpeace; it brings disaster. The hopeless opposition it puts up consumes life: to oppose an inner calling

Heb. 3:14–18

means death. Sin, as separation, is our ruin. In fact, its very nature is opposition to God, without whom we cannot live.

Peace of heart is founded on unity with God. There is no peace when we are far from him. The soul must become quiet, wanting to receive the hidden influence of God in silence. Only then can arise the strength of inner peace ready for deeds. Only when all our attention is concentrated on God can warmth-giving energy come over us, without which we sink

1 John 2:5–11

into cold and darkness. Tersteegen emphasized that an active life must be subordinated to inner quiet so that the soul never gives out more than it takes in.[18] Those who lead an active and fruitful life need time in which all they are and do becomes silent so that

---

17 Johann Heinrich Pestalozzi, 1746–1827, "Die Abendstunde eines Einsiedlers," *Ephemeriden der Menschheit,* May 1780.

18 Gerhard Tersteegen, 1697–1769, German Reformed writer of hymns and religious works.

God can speak and act in the depths of their souls. It is in the very center of our spirit that the words of peace must have an effect. Outside in the clamor of our work, we can all too often fail to hear them.

Isa. 30:15

The words of the great peace bringer, Jesus, that the heavily laden soul shall find rest with him, with the further counsel to pray in secret, have led many to take on the character of "those who are quiet in the land." Some groups call themselves "the silent ones" or "those who have achieved peace and quiet in this life." Yet there often creeps in a much too human tendency to ignore the basic will of Jesus: that inner gathering should become the source of strength for action. To sink spinelessly into a dumb stillness means being lost to the life to which Jesus has called us.

Matt. 11:28–29
Matt. 6:6
Ps. 35:20
Ps. 37:7
1 Thess. 4:9–11

Eph. 3:16–21

Even Augustine was not always free of the old danger of ascetic detachment and withdrawal from life.[19] The way to joy as he saw it was that the soul and all its powers of imagination become so silent that the soul itself is swept away and engulfed in its own oblivion. Such a withdrawal – a "disinterested love," as Fénelon calls it – is nothing less than self-sought death.[20] Then it is not into God and his kingdom that the soul wants to sink but into the nothingness of nirvana.

Self-examination before God never dulls or stupefies; rather, it brings about the liveliest concentration of all energies. It is a regenerating mineral bath, clarifying judgment and strengthening character. God is personal and holy will. There is nothing of

---

19 Augustine of Hippo, 354–430, bishop and theologian.

20 François de Salignac de la Mothe-Fénelon, 1651–1715, Catholic archbishop, theologian, and poet.

a gloomy, all-engulfing abyss about him. The dark
morass of our subconscious, the depths of our own
soul, is not the God who redeems us. It is nothing
but the fathomless mirror of our own self and all our
experiences, good and bad. God, the wholly other
God, wants to illuminate this night so that like the
prodigal son we come to our senses and long for – and
actually grasp – the nearness of God, the exposure of
our hidden darkness and the breaking in of light.

Luke 15:11–32

2 Cor. 4:5–6

We must emerge from the tranquility of indifference, passing through the silence of despair to
the holy calm of inner peace. Hildebert of Tours has
expressed it in the following words:

> Behold, a threefold silence, the first proceeding from
> ignorance of need; the second from despair of deliver-
> ance; the third from the calm of restored life. Before
> the law was given man knew not his disease, therefore
> he was silent and asked not help; when the law was
> given, it discovered to him his gaping wounds; the
> silence ceased immediately, and the sick sought safety
> through the works of the law. But all his endeavors
> were vain; with tears and groans he sank into a
> mournful silence. At last came the almighty Word of
> the Father; again the deceitful stillness was broken;
> he spoke of peace, and promised mercy; the sick arose
> on all sides, and, as with one voice, petitioned eagerly
> that great Physician to save their souls. Once restored
> to perfect health, they will no longer need such
> entreaty. Then shall commence that third silence
> which shall endure even unto eternity.[21]

Rom. 7:6–11

Matt. 9:18–38

---

21 Hildebert of Lavardin, Archbishop of Tours, 1055–1133, in *Spiritual Voices
from the Middle Ages* (London: Joseph Masters, 1865), 30.

Nevertheless the third silence of worship (as the active peace of the kingdom of God) is productive quiet, coming from creative life-energy. It leads to undreamed-of power and influence, which formerly was obstructed in every way. Whoever has gone through depths of misery knows the cause of the sickness that robs him of strength and paralyzes his activity. As David describes it: "There is no rest in my bones because of my sin!" But he is permitted to find healing. God has paved the way even for the most burdened. Ps. 38:3–9

Over this world of sharp inner contrasts and conflicting storms, the colorful rainbow of God's peace is spanned. His mystery is that he reveals his heart as the will for love, through which he transforms the clouds of judgment into unveiled light. Without the storms of judgment, the sun's rainbow cannot be formed. Only he can bring it who is himself without darkness, but who has nevertheless taken the clouds of judgment upon his own life of light so that in it we may see the rainbow of peace. Ezek. 1:26–28

Jesus is our peace

Jesus is our peace. He has brought us complete reconciliation and union with God. His death is the gospel of peace, for he brings death to the sins through which we were excluded from unity. The gift of grace has set peace over and against division. All who receive Christ as their conciliator have peace with God. Through Christ's cross, what had hindered us and removed us from God's influence has been swept away. Through the indwelling Christ, the heart submits to the rulership of God. It has won through Eph. 2

Isa. 53:4–5

Isa. 9:6–7

Heb. 7:1–3

1 John 1:7

to unity in the will of God. Whoever is one with God
has peace. God is peace. The Son of his atonement is
the ruler of peace; as the king of joy, he is called the
King of Peace.

When his gospel of peace reaches the heart, God
in his overwhelming light exposes everything that
has hindered harmony and made it impossible. Inner
gathering is possible only when all sources of division
have been rendered powerless. The essence of all
inner division, the hindrance to peace, is separation
and resistance. Sin is enmity and disbelief. Serving
peace has one goal: to establish the obedience of faith
so that everything trying to hinder and destroy unity
with God is abolished.

Inner turmoil precedes inner peace

Firsthand accounts show clearly how inner peace
overcomes division. August Hermann Francke was
a man whose inner peace brought forth a creative
power of love effective up to the present day. One day,
in great fear, unbelief, and despair, he had called on
the God he did not know. His prayer was answered
so suddenly that peace flooded his heart like a river
inundating the land before anyone has time to realize
that the dike has broken:

> For in the twinkling of an eye, all my doubts were
> gone; I was assured in my heart of the grace of God
> in Christ Jesus; I could call God not only "God" but
> also "my Father." At once all the sadness and unrest
> of my heart was taken away; I was suddenly over-
> whelmed by such a flood of joy that I praised God
> with a full heart for showing me such great grace.
> When I got up, I was in a completely different frame

of mind from when I knelt down. For I had bent my
knees in great distress and doubt, but I got up in
great certainty and unspeakable joy.[22]

Research into religious experience has confirmed that
peace is inevitably preceded by turmoil and doubt.
The first thing that drives the conscience toward
peace is the agony of a bad conscience, a conscious-
ness of sin that grips the soul. At the same time,   Luke 18:13–14
the desperate longing for purity and perfection, for
harmony and community with God, drives the heart   Ps. 42
on to peace, like a storm before the calm.

A burdened conscience may not always be ascribed
to obvious offenses that give generally accepted
morals a slap in the face. More often it is the depress-
ing conviction of an all-pervading disharmony and
bondage to guilt that has its origin in separation from
God. The whole of human life today is "sinfulness"; it
lacks entirely the joy of peace, the strength of justice, Rom. 3:10–18
and the uniting works of God.

Starbuck has made a collection from numerous
accounts of such experiences.[23] He says that the inner
turmoil preceding the state of peace is essentially a
despairing consciousness of sin combined with the
striving toward a new and better life. A crushing
sense of doubt and alienation from God leads to
pessimism and sadness, to deep-seated fear and helplessness. The more we give way to intellectual doubt,
the more effort we make to resist the consciousness

---

22 August Hermann Francke, 1663–1727, quoted in Carl Becker, *August
Hermann Franke: Ein Mann nach dem Herzen Gottes* (Hermannsburg:
Missionshausbuchdruckerei, 1879).

23 Edwin Diller Starbuck, 1866–1947, *The Psychology of Religion: An
Empirical Study of the Growth of the Religious Consciousness* (London: Walter
Scott, 1899).

of guilt and the greater grows the agony. Fear, doubt, and a sense of sin and depression are the throes of the coming birth.

Rebirth brings inner peace

This new birth is the narrow gate to the kingdom of peace. Inner peace is seized hold of as liberation, freedom from the gloom of sin, and redemption from the curse. In this birth, we come into the new world and see the kingdom of God. The more keenly we feel the contrast between our weakness and helplessness on the one hand and the power and glory on the other as the contrast between man and God, the more powerfully does all that is new show itself. God's cause takes the place of man and his misery. The peace of the coming kingdom brings with it forgiveness for division and sin, and harmony with God's power of love. All energies formerly squandered by the will are from now on directed toward God and his kingdom in a new, previously unknown clarity. As in war we felt more strongly the blessings of peace, so peace of heart depends on the intensity of its contrast to sin, disharmony, feebleness, and disruptedness. Life can arise only in this tension between our torn and feeble state and the energy of God's peace.

For this reason Paul was told, "My grace is sufficient for you, for my power is made perfect in weakness," and Luther said, "God is the God of the humble, the miserable, the afflicted. It is His nature to exalt the humble, to comfort the sorrowing, to heal the broken-hearted, to justify the sinners, and to save the condemned."[24]

Matt. 7:13–14

John 3:2–8

Luke 7:47–50

2 Cor. 12:9–10

24 Martin Luther, *Commentary on the Epistle to the Galatians.*

It is God's nature to show his superior power just where darkness and weakness have destroyed the last hope. "Where sin increased, grace increased all the more." It is God's will that our own strength be broken. In its morbid self-love and within its own narrow confines, human strength is bound to exhaust itself utterly. But the end of our own strength is the beginning of the other: the birth of faith begins. Faith presses on to God's love, to the future of his kingdom. From faith, love arises as love to God and Christ put into practice: joy in God's creation and in other people, joyful and confident expectation of God's kingdom, unity with the church of Jesus Christ, and the life of God's new creation. Utterly new and unexpected, this life comes over the believers as Jesus' words being surprisingly fulfilled: to give up oneself means to win life. A new life, God's true life, replaces the former selfish and ungenuine life. Whoever loves his life loses it; whoever hates his life receives true life.

Rom. 5:20

John 15:10–11

John 12:24–26

The new life is an undivided whole – perfection that exists in God alone. The previous life let two irreconcilably opposed egos exist side by side: the "I" as it is and the "I" as it is meant to be. Through peace of heart, an undivided will dedicated to the new life allows the holy "shall be" to triumph over the unholy "is." "God will be born in us only when all the bound and captive powers of our soul become entirely free, when all our plans and ideas are silenced, and when our conscience ceases to punish us."[25] All plans and ideas disappear into the inner imperative of the holy "thou shalt," and the soul experiences unity and freedom. It is the freedom of obedience on which the

Rom. 7:14–23

---

25 Meister Eckhart, ca. 1260–ca. 1328, Sermon 25.

peace of Christmas depends; the cause of this birth
is what brings peace. Mary believed. She obeyed. The
Spirit came. Christ was born.

Mary listened to the word and treasured it in her
heart. The word given to the prophets said, "If only
you had paid attention to my commands, your peace
would have been like a river." The flood of the Spirit
penetrates to the depths. The riverbed is saturated
deep into hidden ground. Though the level of the
water may rise or fall, in the deepest depths there
is abundance. The peace of God penetrates into the
depths. Without these depths, all religious exercises
and Christian forms are nothing but a delusion: mists
but no river. Action begins in the inmost heart and
then penetrates far into all areas of life. The water
Jesus gives is from a well of depth.

The inmost depths are decisive; Jesus exposes the
heart. He directs his glance to what is going on there.
He lays his finger on it, for he sees things as they really
are. "He knew what was in each person." He made
this clear: what rules in our hearts gains control over
our lives. "A good man brings forth good from the
goodness stored in his heart; a bad man brings forth
evil from the evil stored in his heart." "It is out of the
abundance of the heart that the mouth speaks." As the
heart, so is the deed: peace of heart brings about a life
of peace. The Spirit of Jesus affects the inmost depths
first and foremost: "Let the peace of God reign in your
hearts." "The peace of God will keep your hearts and
your minds. It surpasses all understanding. It keeps
and preserves you in Christ Jesus."

The word of peace penetrates to the depths. The
living Word brings about a living peace: "What I

Luke 1:26–38

Isa. 48:18

John 4:14

John 2:23–25

Matt. 12:34–35
Luke 6:45

Col. 3:15

Phil. 4:7

have said, I have told you so that in me you may have peace!" Through being kept in the heart, the word becomes deed, which is the bedrock of the unity of peace. Peace exists in Jesus because through his life and deeds community with God is given. The life of Jesus leads us to the wellsprings of inner strength and shows us the way this strength is overwhelmingly at work right to the end of the world, to the final goal of all time.

John 16:33

Matt. 7:24–29

Inner quiet gives strength for activity
Jesus hid himself from the multitudes on the secluded heath, on the lonely mountain, and in the quiet boat. He loved peaceful solitude for his communion with God. He loved to gather his strength in God's quiet. He spent whole nights talking with him. Contemplative quiet, however, was never Jesus' goal; it was his source of living works and strength for his heavy task. Out of this quiet he went to the people. Coming out of his solitude, he gathered thousands to him and advanced to the big city. His mission goes out into all the world. His love heals bodies and saves souls. His was a life of active love that needed the power of gathered concentration in order to reach the widest circles. In quiet before God, he gained the strength for each advance right up to the last battle – his bitter death.

Matt. 14:13–23

Mark 1:35–39

Matt. 26:36–46

The peace of Jesus is altogether different from a mood of impassive withdrawal. Without God we may try to force a false peace of soul, a placid repose. The cool tranquility of a selfishly withdrawn life is far removed from the peace of God. God works a different peace: one that comes from having a confident spirit and, out of a full life, works for our ultimate calling – the all-embracing kingdom! A God-conscious life becomes a source of rich activity. When the heart is filled from its deepest depths, there is a well-grounded certainty that the Crucified One is the one and only source of a peace that is both inmost and all-embracing. The Crucified One rooted out sin, which had allowed no peace to grow, and he does the work of peace in creating perfect unity.

As fresh water in a river continues to flow hour after hour, so the peace of God lives in the continuously renewed experience of Christ at work within us. Christ wants to remain in us so that even in the greatest need and distress we do the same works of peace as he did. Just as cloudbursts and torrents of rain widen and deepen a riverbed, so times of severe storm and violent unrest will serve to deepen and strengthen peace. Need and misery should lead us to that final state of determination which the scriptures call repentance. Godly sadness and fruitful remorse bring forth peace, the good fruit of repentance. No sudden storm can change the character of peace. Storms merely test and confirm it. There may be waves on the surface of the water that make it appear as if the current were flowing backward. But the direction of the current does not change: the main body of water goes forward unperturbed.

Peace strengthens. Courage that comes from peace is without fear. God's plan of peace for us does not anticipate suffering without the courage of joy. Peace, as community with Christ, is a fruit of the same Spirit as joy and patience. The spiritual fruit of peace is a love that builds up in brotherliness. Its power

Ps. 51:10–15

Gal. 2:20

John 17

Ps. 46:1–5

2 Cor. 7:8–11

John 14:27

Gal. 5:22–23

is the kingdom of justice. "What is sown by peace becomes the fruit of righteousness." The kingdom of God, in the church of this age as well as in the ultimate future, is "justice and peace and joy in the Holy Spirit."

James 3:18

Rom. 14:17–18

The kingdom of God in our hearts is the foundation of God's rulership over the whole earth and over all worlds. The peace of the church of Jesus Christ is commissioned as a forerunner of the peace of the future and of all eternity. Francis of Assisi used to begin each talk and each encounter with "Peace be with you," and the Hutterians in their daily life in full community also greeted each other with "Peace be with you."[26] So also today we must confront the unpeace of the whole world with these words of true brotherhood: "You must proclaim peace. Cherish it in your own hearts. See to it that through the life you share together in love, all shall be led to concord and unity – to the creative and openhearted justice of peace!"

Acts 9:31

Dan. 7:18, 22, 27

---

26 The Hutterites are an Anabaptist group that started in the sixteenth century. Arnold was deeply impressed by their witness of full community and modeled the Bruderhof on their example; in 1931, he was ordained as a minister in the Hutterian Church.